COURAGEOUS
COMMUNICATION

by
MARYANNE DERSCH

COURAGEOUS
COMMUNICATION

How Codependence
Is Making Your
Nonprofit Brand Boring
and WHEN TO DO ABOUT IT

by
MARYANNE DERSCH

STONEBROOK
PUBLISHING

Stonebrook Publishing
Saint Louis, Missouri

Acknowledgments

had about sixteen panic attacks while I was writing this book. It's never easy to share your truth, and even though this book is about this very topic, it's still hard.

I want to thank that girl in college who asked me a question that haunted me for years (sorry, I don't remember your name!). She asked, "What are you going to do with all this social justice stuff when you go into advertising?" I thought that was the stupidest question anyone could ever ask. What does my racial justice, shantytown self (it was the 80s!) have to do with my advertising self? Turns out, it was a lot. She was the first person in my life to notice the gap and the only person to call it out. Thank you, friend.

I tried to write this book for years before I met Nancy Erickson, The Book Professor. Thank you, Nancy, for taking something difficult and daunting and making it digestible and attainable.

Thank you to my longtime career coach, Shary Raske. Shary helped me find my nonprofit path all the way back in 1992, and I'm grateful for her professional expertise and personal friendship over the years. She made me see that I can shape my life into anything I want it to be.

Thank you to my boss and friend, Karen Handelman, who was not only foolish enough to hire me but also let me use my workspace and computer to write this book. Also, thank you for being a badass editor and creative partner.

Thank you to Sue Bechmann at *501creative* for helping me create a visual identity.

Thank you to my colleagues, clients, and professional friends who served as stories for this book. Your work inspires me and fills me with life. I love what I do, and I love knowing all of you.

Thank you to my family and friends for loving and supporting me along this journey. Writing a book is scary and weird and hard. You were all wonderful and encouraging and all the things you want people you love to be.

And finally, thank you to my husband, Jon Schmuke. You married a wild one, and it never deterred you. I can't do anything the way anyone else does, and I'm glad you find that quality endearing. Thank you for letting me ruin countless carpets with unhousetrained foster dogs. Thank you for building our family through foster care. I'm not sure if you knew what you were getting into when you married me, but thank you for sticking around long enough to find out.

Contents

What Is Courageous Communication?

've been doing it all wrong. As a brand consultant, coach, teacher, and writer—along with my experience with cognitive behavior therapy—I now understand that teaching people communication tools is wrong. I can teach you how to write compelling web content or develop an engaging brand, but unless you have the courage to do that, nothing will change. I've been treating the *symptoms*, not the *disease*.

I call it the "Biggest Loser Syndrome." I can put you on a restricted diet and work you out five hours a day, but it won't help you understand how you got to four hundred pounds in the first place.

We've been treating the behaviors rather than how we *think* and *feel*, which influences behavior.

In order to communicate effectively, we need to change how we *feel*, which changes our thoughts and then changes our behaviors. If we *think* our nonprofit organizations are smart, stable, interesting, confident, and strong, then our communications will achieve better results. We must look at the *thinking* and *feeling* first, and then the *behavior*.

My goal is to help you manage your feelings, so you can change your thoughts, which will make you more courageous and bold—and you'll care a lot less about what people think. Believe it or not, when you need less praise and are able to manage criticism, you'll attract more people to you, not less. This is the heart of courageous communication.

Let's say that again: when you care less about what people think, you'll gain supporters.

I *know*! It does sound crazy, counterintuitive, and kind of dangerous. But hang with me.

We Are Codependent Nightmares

What does codependency mean? It means you sacrifice your own needs for the needs of others. Those of us in helper professions are this way by nature. We want to do for others and make the world a better place. The issue, however, is *at what cost?* If we constantly put what we need behind the needs of others, then we're going to suffer.

That makes sense, right? Put on your own oxygen mask before you help someone else with theirs. That's a challenge for us, and particularly for nonprofits.

Nonprofits have relationships with their donors, and they're based on an exchange of value. We give our donors something they value, and they give us something in return. Our "something of value" is to work on issues our donors care about that they don't have the time, money, or expertise to handle. For example, I can't rescue *every* dog, although I'd love to try. And Stray Rescue of Saint Louis does a much better job than I do. I give them money; they get the dogs.

Sometimes the exchange is hard to measure, and it's a challenge to believe we're equal to our donors because we need their dollars. Thus, we feel dependent on our donors. We don't feel like the relationship is equal.

This is where the "co" is added to the "dependence."

We want to make everyone happy. We're terrified of criticism. We don't take a stand lest we anger someone or disappoint a donor. We hold back on social media because we're afraid someone will post a negative comment. We've said "no" to an interview or to inviting a speaker for an event because we thought they might ruffle feathers. That's why our brands tend to be pretty *blah*—because we want to please everyone. But when we try to appeal to everyone, we stand out to no one.

Cognitive behavior therapy, which is the basis for some of these principles, tells us that praise and criticism are the same thing. How can this be? It's because we shouldn't need either one to feel good or bad about ourselves. We shouldn't be dependent on praise to make us happy, and criticism shouldn't send us over the edge.

A good leader will have a specific point of view and stick to it, whether they receive praise or criticism. It's not that they're immune to feedback; they just make it work for them without getting derailed.

When we're so afraid of criticism that it gets in the way of our ability to share our message, that's codependence. I see it all the time, so if this rings true, you're not alone.

> A good leader will have a specific point of view and stick to it, whether they receive praise or criticism. It's not that they're immune to feedback; they just make it work for them without getting derailed.

To be strong in your message, you must understand who you are as an organization and accept that. You won't appeal to everyone. And those people who get upset? Come on, they weren't really on board anyway. Your true supporters want an authentic relationship. You can tell them the good, the bad, and everything in between, and they'll love you all the more for it.

Together, we're going to explore how organizations become codependent, how you can find your authentic message, and how you can use it to engage loyal, long-term donors. I swear. It's true.

Being Authentic Is Worth the Risk

Imagine your organization is a person. What is it like? Is it confident, capable, interesting, and committed? Or is it tentative, insecure, and boring? If you knew someone who needed as much approval as your nonprofit and had only wonderful, flowery things to say, you'd avoid that person at all costs. That's what we sound like—one long, bragging holiday letter. "Everything is so wonderful. We are so awesome. Please support our awesomeness."

> Imagine your organization is a person. What is it like? Is it confident, capable, interesting, and committed? Or is it tentative, insecure, and boring?

You've seen this very thing on social media. I believe that the more a couple talks about how much they love each other on Facebook the more miserable the relationship. Can they really be that happy all the time? No, they can't! I can smell the inauthenticity and you can, too. Let's not be that.

Real relationships are formed when we're honest and authentic. Donors want to know us because they're people just like us, and they want the truth. But we're afraid to show our truths because we think the risks are too high.

The risk of being boring and bland is that you'll be overlooked. This is a competitive world. How can we compete with the cute video of the momma cat who let the orphaned puppy nurse alongside her kittens, or the latest Donald Trump meme, or another one of those Delish recipe videos?

4

We must be able to hold interest, which we can't do if we say only good stuff all the time. We have to have a point of view. We have to be part of conversations that we didn't start. We have to stand up for what we believe.

> We can't hold peoples' interest if we say only good stuff all the time. We have to have a point of view. We have to be a part of conversations that we didn't start. We have to stand up for what we believe.

You may remember in April of 2017, a Miami police officer shot at a man with autism and his caregiver, mistaking the man's toy train for a weapon. It was all over Facebook. The story was hard to miss. Well, for my friends Pamela and Crystal Merritt, this story is their personal nightmare. Their older brother, Bill, is autistic. His public behaviors, although normal for Bill, can be seen as difficult or threatening to others. The fact that his behavior might be interpreted as violent is their greatest fear. I paid attention to what Pamela was saying about this event, and she was calling out Autism Speaks on Twitter, asking for a response. Their Twitter and Facebook feeds said nothing about this event.

Now I know why this was a terrifying issue to address: police shooting, race, disabilities—a real public relations nightmare. But instead of looking at this as a crisis, we could look at this as an opportunity—an opportunity to talk about adults who have austim (kids get most of the attention), how police are trained to interact with people with disabilities, how people who love or care for someone with autism can work with the police. But there was nothing.

I get it; I do. But being courageous calls us to speak up at a time when we are called to do so. Any organization that assists people with autism could have spoken up about this issue. I bring up Autism Speaks because it was the organization my friend was looking to for guidance.

If your organization isn't saying something, someone else will. We were having a national conversation about a very difficult and important issue.

In subsequent months, there was plenty written and said about the event. But the conversation was over, we had moved on to the next event. If an organization had been a part of this conversation, offering its views on what happened and the lessons to be learned from it, what would have happened? Well, a few people might have been upset, but others would have been grateful for the leadership.

When we stand for something, some people will like it and others won't. But this is the approach that will help you raise more money and gain devoted followers. It goes against everything we've ever been taught as nonprofits. I get that. But if I were saying the same thing as everyone else, I wouldn't need a whole book to explain it.

It's About Everyone Who's Not Reading This Book

You'll learn how to up-sell a change in *thinking*—how to convince those in charge of your nonprofit that courageous communicators attract people to you rather than drive them away. I know my fine counterparts in nonprofits realize they need to create content that has a strong message in order to hold interest and compel people to action; but man-oh-man, how do you convince that buttoned up board that it's OK to do that?

> I won't teach you how to do things differently; instead, I'll teach you how to think differently and how to teach your organization to think differently. That's what has to happen to put new ideas in place.

I won't teach you how to do things differently; instead, I'll teach you how to *think* differently and how to teach *your organization* to think differently. That's what has to happen to put new ideas in place. Without a shift in thought, new ideas and strategies are simply an exercise in frustration.

Get Off the Attention Treadmill and Get Results

If you want to make time stand still, jump on a treadmill. Longest forty-five minutes of my life. I work hard and go nowhere. If your communications program sounds like a treadmill, let's think about changing your approach so you can move forward.

Many years ago, our typical approach to marketing was "spray and pray": spread lots of messages and hope someone saw or heard and responded. That method wasn't very efficient or effective. Who even read that newsletter? What did our supporters need? Unless they told us, we didn't know, because we couldn't gauge their behaviors.

Today, we have so many tools to connect with our supporters. We can see what emails they open, what they forward, read, share, etc. Thanks to this information, we can hone in on our best prospects.

Our approach needs to shift. To convince everyone that your organization is worthy and valuable when most of them don't become supporters is a waste of time, energy, and money. The new approach is to find like-minded people and be available to them, so they're attracted to your organization. Get off the treadmill. It's time to stand still and be available and easy to find. Instead of spreading your message and hoping someone responds, stand tall in your message and make your organization easy to find. Then when people who are interested in your cause go looking, there you are! And because they have self-identified as being interested, you already know they think you are worthy and valuable.

Find People Who Already Care

We all have our own personal philanthropic wheelhouse. I rescue things. It's what I do. It's as hardwired in me as wearing high heels. I'm not a flats or flip-flops girl, and you can't make me wear them. Leggings aren't pants, and you can't convince me they are. So stop trying!

Same with my personal mission: I'm a rescuer. My kids are all adopted from foster care. My family and I have fostered more than 140 dogs for Stray Rescue of Saint Louis. It's not that I don't care about seniors, or diabetes, or addiction; it's that those causes aren't in my wheelhouse. You can push, pull, or tug, but I won't change. I'm not going to start wearing ballet flats. It won't happen. Your attempts to convince me otherwise are a waste of time and energy.

Your job isn't to convince people that your cause is worthy. Instead, just be strong in your message and easy to find. Have solid SEO rankings and an up-to-date website. Blog, post, tweet, and share messages that connect you to those who think like you. Then your qualified prospects, volunteers, and programs can find you, and you already know they're interested.

It seems weird not to chase after prospects—like you're not doing your job. But when you share stories of value and interest and you're helpful, available, and can be found, people will respond. It will get you off the treadmill and get you results.

For Further Thought

- Name some of the codependent behaviors in your organization.

- From what you now know of courageous communication, what are your barriers to adopting these principles?

- How could being a more courageous communicator benefit your organization?

I'M A CODEPENDENT NIGHTMARE:
I Know the Territory

As a child, I felt a little left out because I was what my parents called a "Michelob baby." At the time, Michelob's slogan was "The Unexpected Pleasure." Six years younger than my closest sibling, eleven years younger than the oldest, I felt like the family footnote. I was a baby when they were kids. When I was a kid, they were teens. When I was a teen, they lived on their own. I often told people I was an only child with three moms and three dads. Now, of course, I love all of them so much and we're very close, but when I was growing up, it was hard for me to feel like I had value. My sisters were prettier; my brothers were cooler. I sort of hung around waiting to be noticed.

This position in my family is where my career in codependence started. I understand what it's like to feel left out. As a result, I was always the first one to make friends with the new kid in school, the first to befriend the shy kid. We may not have stayed friends, but I was the one who paved the way.

> This position in my family is where my career in codependence started. I understand what it's like to feel left out.

I grew up in a very white, Catholic school, and I worked on social justice issues there, even though I had no experience with poverty or racial injustice. College was much the same. I was in journalism school as an advertising major. It was what my dad did, and I loved it because I loved to come up with ideas.

One day in school, a fellow student asked me what I was going to do with all this social justice passion when I went to work at an advertising agency. I thought that was the stupidest question anyone could ask. What was she even talking about? It didn't take me long to figure out that I didn't care if you bought Budweiser or Miller (now produced by the same company, as my dad rolls in his grave). I didn't care about commercial products. I cared about people, about making their lives better.

After a first disaster of a job in the art department of a plastics company, I started working in nonprofits and have never looked back. For six years I worked as a public relations person inside a local government; then for four years I was a consultant for a company that developed communications plans and managed public engagement for nonprofits, civic groups, and government agencies. This grueling work taught me how to develop processes in order to make good decisions. Then I went to work at *501creative*, where we provide strategic, creative solutions for nonprofit organizations. I work with nonprofits on communications plans, brands, design, web development, and campaign work.

But all these years later, I'm still the same girl who cried at the top of the driveway when all my siblings rode their bikes to the convenience store. I was only four, so it probably wasn't a good idea for me to tag along, even in the early seventies when safety was not a big concern. But I still felt left behind.

I still struggle with a badass case of Fear of Missing Out (FOMO). If my friends are at a bar without me, I think they must hate me! If my siblings had an outing and I didn't go, even though it didn't interest me or I couldn't have made it anyway, I feel sad. I know this is a fundamental part of me and that my FOMO won't disappear. But now I know how to manage it more effectively.

My career and my life are dedicated to helping those on the margins, to bringing them into the fold. I foster dogs, and my kids are adopted out of foster care. I rescue nonprofits from bad communications. I help them figure out their worth, build up their sense of who they are and why they matter, and share that message with people who care about them and their issues.

All organizations have strengths to share. They all have relationships of value. They just need some help to get there. It's hard to cut through the clutter and see your organization from the outside. I get it. When you're so entrenched, it's hard to take a step back.

> All organizations have strengths they can share. They all have relationships they can value. They just need some help to get there.

This is what I do. I come in wearing my big platform shoes and my larger-than-life personality, and I fire you up. I get you to see your assets, your strengths, and what you do that's better than any other organization. Then I help you find audiences that value those things, and we create strong relationships with them. It's about building bridges—to the new kid at school, to my older siblings, to my clients to help them move to a better place. It's about building bridges between the organizations I work with and their audiences.

If you're going to grow, you need to change. But how do you do that? How do you communicate better? How do you reach the people you need to reach?

For Further Thought

- Write down some examples of how you are codependent.

- Brainstorm and then write down your organizational mission.

YOU CAN'T BORE THEM INTO ACTION:
How to Create Compelling Messages

I am a burlesque dancer. At fifty-one, I decided the logical choice for me was to adopt a hobby where I take off my clothes in public. And I love it! What I love about this culture is that there are no rules other than you must be entertaining. You can be any shape, sex, or have any odd talent you want. Your act can be sexy, funny, scary, or poignant. But you better be entertaining.

Burlesque has taught me to tell a compelling story in a short period of time and to make the audience believe that story. Take them on a journey. Shock them, move them, or humor them. Above all, make them *feel something*.

Compelling Messages

In order for people to listen to you and your messages about your organization, you need to know who you are and what you want to say. You also have to make your audience feel something.

This is a special challenge for nonprofits. In order to get people's attention, you have to say something interesting. And to capture their interest, you need to say something of value. And yet, we often recoil at that thought lest it cause controversy or anger, or, heaven forbid, we look so silly that it seems like we don't take our mission seriously. When we're afraid of being too controversial or too flighty, we create safe, sound, and happy messages that don't move people to action.

We are a snooze fest. People don't pay attention because we don't give them anything to pay attention to. We play it safe. And then we wonder why no one pays attention to us.

> We are a snooze fest. People don't pay attention because we don't give them anything to pay attention to. And then we wonder why no one pays attention to us.

While I was giving a workshop with fundraising consultants, one participant said that her client was afraid to share content that could be perceived as negative. I thought, *How can you make an appeal to give to your cause if you can't admit you need to improve your organization?* Fear kept this group from making a strong case for campaign funds.

This fear is real and valid, and it can thwart our ability to communicate directly and raise money.

In order to find new supporters and keep our current ones, we need to generate attention. How can we do that?

The Communications Pyramid

Your Brand Promise—the Soul of Your Organization

The first step to courageous communications is to develop a brand promise. A brand promise, or a brand statement, or a unique sales proposition (marketing is famous for different words that mean the same thing!), is how the organization makes a high-level connection with its customers. It's the promise that says, "We know you and we understand you."

COMMUNICATIONS PYRAMID

Brand Promise

Main Message

Description

Talking Points

Short Stories

Long Stories

Outcomes

Target's brand promise to its customers—and this is a personal interpretation, but I spend a lot of time in Target stores—is *to have a great experience*. For many women, going to Target is a recreational activity. When my oldest child joined our family at three years old, I was overwhelmed. To calm myself and pass the time, I would push him around Target just for fun. I figured if I was happy, he'd be happy! And I was happy in Target.

Target never says, "Have a great experience," but it's the unspoken promise they make through their advertising and their atmosphere. Compare that to Walmart. They aren't very concerned about your experience because their brand promise is to save you money, which also appeals to many shoppers.

A brand promise creates an emotional connection. It says, "We understand you, and we are here to meet your needs."

We start with this connection and then build from there. The heart comes first, then the mind, then the wallet. Establishing an emotional connection is key to forming a relationship—in our personal lives, as well as with our donors.

How do you develop a brand promise? You must first understand your organization and probe those who are involved across your different audiences—staff, board, volunteers, and donors. Why do they love you? Why are they connected to you?

To find out, ask them questions that get to the heart of their connection, such as:

- What first attracted you to this organization?

- Why do you love us?

- What do you tell your friends or colleagues about us?

Listen for common themes. Look for the strongest, deepest emotional connection. When you have an idea or two, run it by a small group of people to see their reaction. You'll know if you're getting close.

The benefit of a solid brand promise is that the whole organization and all your communications can be built on that connection. It allows your communications to be focused and relevant to your audiences.

Main Message: Share Why Your Audience Should Care

A main message is an audience-directed statement that describes the benefit of your organization. It is *not* a mission statement, which is an internal statement that gives an organization direction. Call it a tagline, a phrase, or a main message, but the function is the same: it answers the question, "Why should I care about your organization?"

Look for balance in your main message. If your organization's name tends to be descriptive or a little dry, the main message can add emotion and heart. If your name is emotional or a little hard to understand, use the main message to clarify your purpose.

> A main message is an audience-directed statement that describes the benefit of your organization.

For many years, *501creative* has worked with Oasis Institute, a national organization with chapters all over the country. Oasis provides educational, health, and volunteer opportunities to older adults. The issue is that "oasis" is the name for a lot of things—a British rock band, a pool cleaning company, a spa. When *501creative* started tackling this issue, we needed a main message that clarified the purpose of the organization and gave it some heart.

And here was the other kicker: no labels allowed. *Seniors* and *older adults* were no-no words. During a two-hour brainstorm session, we explored the brand promise. What we were promising was the idea of being young at heart, of being active, engaged, and interested throughout life. Here's what we came up with:

Oasis: Lifelong Adventure

This short message tells who it's for (lifelong learners) and why (adventure) without the messy *senior* or other age-related words.

It worked! It also works well as a directive—*your* lifelong adventure—in ads and other materials.

Descriptions: Make It Easy to Tell What You Do

Taglines or main messages are a great tool, but we don't really talk in taglines. A description answers the question, "Who are we?"

Oasis promotes healthy aging through lifelong learning, active lifestyles, and volunteer engagement.

When someone asks what your organization does, don't answer with a laundry list of services and programs. A description tells a story of who you are and why you matter.

Here's another example of a description for a nonprofit I worked with, Community Living:

Community Living enriches the lives of people with disabilities, so they can achieve their highest potential. We provide children and adults with services, so they can live, learn, and work in our community. In turn, they make our community inclusive, diverse and a better place to live.

Talking Points: Tailor Your Message to Your Audiences

A brand promise, main message, and description put you on a great path, but you need to go further and establish talking points. Talking points allow you to tailor your messages to your audiences, and they answer four questions:

- **Who we are:** This is your agency description. The description remains constant and is *not* tailored to any audience because who you are as an organization doesn't change, no matter the audience.

- **How we do it:** This speaks to your processes, such as the programs and services you offer that achieve what you stated in your agency description. This also remains constant.

- **Why you should care:** This is audience-directed. Your talking points will be tailored to each audience because each audience has different reasons to care about what you do. Corporations may care about sales, and donors may care about recognition. Your talking points to these diverse audiences are completely different.

- **What to do about it:** This is a call to action that's tailored to each of your audiences.

Here's an example from Community Living:

TALKING POINTS

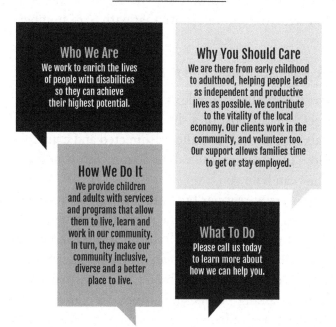

Who We Are
We work to enrich the lives of people with disabilities so they can achieve their highest potential.

Why You Should Care
We are there from early childhood to adulthood, helping people lead as independent and productive lives as possible. We contribute to the vitality of the local economy. Our clients work in the community, and volunteer too. Our support allows families time to get or stay employed.

How We Do It
We provide children and adults with services and programs that allow them to live, learn and work in our community. In turn, they make our community inclusive, diverse and a better place to live.

What To Do
Please call us today to learn more about how we can help you.

- **Who we are:** Community Living, Inc. enriches the lives of people with disabilities, so they can achieve their highest potential.

- **How we do it:** We provide children and adults with services, so they can live, learn, and work in our community.

- **Why you should care:** We make your community inclusive, diverse, and a better place to live.

- **What to do about it:** Donate, volunteer, etc.

Outcomes

Outcomes are the data points that prove your talking points are valid. You may be surprised to find these farther down the pyramid, but data works best in context. Audiences understand who you are, why you do what you do, and why they should care. Now you can prove that with hard numbers.

Stories: Bring Your Messages to Life

A *short story* can be as simple as a photo with a caption. It can be a social media post or a short video. But it must relate to your talking points. It is audience-directed and contains a call to action. Don't forget the call to action! Tell your audiences how they can help you.

Long stories are similar, but by nature they're longer because they're used on your website or in printed materials. Again, don't forget the call to action. Tell your readers how they can help and what their actions mean to the organization.

When you develop your brand promise, main message, description, talking points, and stories, you are well on your way to clear and effective communication. Now let's talk about how to share those messages.

Use the Loyalty Index

If you've known someone for a long time, but she approached you as if you'd just met, that might confuse you. Conversely, if you just met someone and she told you something deeply personal, you'd be put off.

This happens to me all the time. I think I have a face that says, "Sit down and tell me all your problems." I'm a journalist by training, and I was taught that everyone has a story, and I do find people genuinely interesting. But people tell me crazy stuff. I recently stopped by my "local" for a drink before meeting my sister for a show, and within five minutes this guy shared his personal pain of being single at age thirty and showed me a picture of his dying grandmother's hand. True story. And this is not an unusual experience for me.

We have innate ways to form relationships that we often don't talk about but we can certainly feel. There is an accepted path, and if we veer off the path, we know it. Perhaps there's something about me that invites people to overshare, but in marketing, we need to step more carefully.

> We have innate ways to form relationships that we often don't talk about but we can certainly feel. There is an accepted path, and if we veer off the path, we know it.

We need to build relationships with our audiences with those innate steps in mind. You wouldn't ask someone to marry you on the first date, and most likely you wouldn't ask a donor for a big gift the first time you meet. Our messages need to honor our audiences and where they are in a relationship with us.

What I call the loyalty index is shown on the next page. Feel free to use it for marketing purposes but also in relationships in general.

There's a new restaurant opening up. Let's use that as an example of how the loyalty index works.

23

LOYALTY INDEX

Unaware	Doesn't know about the organization
Awareness	Learn about the organization
Initiate	Feels positive about the organization
1st Contact	First try or personal contact
2nd Contact	Second try or personal contact
Repeat Contact	Gives to the organization, also gives to other organizations
Loyal Donor	Gives to your organization and no other

- **Unaware:** There's no relationship to a product or organization. I don't know the restaurant exists.

- **Awareness:** I've heard of it but don't have an opinion about it. I drive by and see that it exists.

- **Initiate:** I'm aware of it, have a positive impression, and want to know more. I might look up the restaurant on Yelp, check its website, or save a coupon to use.

- **First contact:** I'm aware of it, have a positive impression, and tried it.

- **Second contact:** I'm aware of it, have a positive impression, tried it, liked it, and am willing to try it again. I had a nice meal and think I would have a nice meal again. Maybe it wasn't perfect, but there were enough positives to get me back.

- **Repeat contact:** I purchase the product but also purchase other products in that same market and will change where I go depending on price, availability, and location. I love the new restaurant, but I still spend my money at other restaurants.

- **Loyal donor:** I purchase only this product regardless of price, availability, location, or any other barrier.

Consider blue jeans. We all wear them. My husband wears only Levi's® 501 jeans—not any other brand or any other style of Levi's® jeans. It doesn't matter that they cost more. He's a loyal consumer. Most of us probably wear several different brands of jeans, which makes us repeat consumers. We might change brands or own several brands depending on fit, cut, style, or price.

How does this work for nonprofits? The same way as for a consumer purchase! Audiences need to know who you are and have a positive impression of you, so they have a reason to initiate contact. And when they do, they need a reason to not only make that first contact, but to make a second contact to become repeat participants.

It's probably not realistic to expect your donors to be *loyal* in the way described above. They might give to several organizations, and that's OK. Most donors who are loyal to nonprofits have a very personal tie. Perhaps they founded it themselves or had a personal experience with the cause or issue. Your sweet spot is in *repeat*.

There are three points to note about this index. First, the person must feel like they're in control the whole time, or they'll bail. If they feel pushed through these relationships, they'll balk.

Ever buy a car and get put in the "box," that stuffy room where you sit while the salesperson runs back and forth to the manager? They try to push you through the process. Cars are loyalty purchases, and they can't afford to let you get away. If you push a supporter for a big commitment without the chance to know you, they'll shut down.

Second, if someone becomes frustrated with the process, they'll shut down, and it will take you twice as long to get them back—if you ever do. For instance, say you get some publicity that generates phone calls, but no one returns those calls. The people did what you wanted—they reached out—but you weren't there to respond. Now they are double mad.

I adopted my kids out of foster care. Here's a fact that might surprise you: there are enough people to adopt kids out of foster care to provide homes for all of them. So what's the problem? The system is so difficult to work with that 94 percent of families that start the process don't adopt. It's because of the unresponsiveness, the bureaucracy, overloaded caseworkers, and other issues.

It typically takes families that think about adopting four or five years to act. And when they finally reach out, they're discouraged because they don't get a call back or can't work through the system. So they say, "I guess that's not for me," and they drop it.

The third point to note about this index is that not everyone is going to progress through it, which is OK. Your job is to find the people most likely to form that repeat relationship, not to convince people to *have* a repeat relationship.

When we don't honor where we are in the relationship, our communications become misguided. Many nonprofits want to target corporations. Well, that's fine, but let's evaluate that according to this index. Where do they fall? How well do they know you? You may need to work on *awareness* and *contact* before you ask them for a commitment.

> Your job is to find the people most likely to form that repeat relationship, not to convince people to have a repeat relationship.

Stop Dating the Bad Boyfriend: Let Go of Relationships That Don't Work For You

We've all had personal, familial, professional, or romantic relationships that didn't feel quite right. You may have felt like you were banging your head against the wall, but it was hard to let go. Trust me, I've been there more than once, and it's painful. But I finally realized that my time and energy needed to be directed elsewhere because the relationship wasn't benefitting either of us. This can happen on the job, with friends, with partners—and it's not a bad thing to walk away. Painful, yes, but bad? Maybe not.

It's the same way with our audiences. Do you spend copious amounts of time and money on people who don't and won't care about you? Do you beat your marketing head against the wall because you don't get more involvement or investment from these groups? Maybe it's time to let them go. Courageous communication is about being honest and authentic in your

> Courageous communication is about being honest and authentic in your words and to whom you communicate. Some audiences aren't worth your time, energy, or money.

words and to whom you communicate. Some audiences aren't worth your time, energy, or money.

Kelly Peach works at St. Patrick Center, an organization in Saint Louis that provides services to people who are homeless or at risk of becoming homeless. A few years ago, they hosted an annual sports trivia night. It was huge. About 1,000 men—and, yes, it was mostly men—filled the field of an indoor stadium to compete. The event raised a lot of money, but like all events, it had its peak and eventually the attendance started to wane. So Kelly decided to change up the event to generate new audiences. Of course, higher-ups were concerned: "We'll lose the sports guys!"

Let's look at that. How many of those sports guys become donors? How many of them care about or supported the issue of homelessness? It was a low conversion rate. All their time and energy was spent on an event to cater to an audience that didn't care much about the organization it supported. Were the sports guys upset? Yes, they were. But that group had reached the peak of its investment. When they introduced a new theme to a new audience, it reenergized the event and allowed for a better pool of potential long-term donors.

Don't be afraid to say goodbye. It's OK. Use data to make your case. How much time and money do you spend and for what return? Figure out where your energy needs to be directed, then detach with love from those who never loved you that much anyway.

What to Say, How Much, and When

When you decide to be courageous, questions will come up. If an issue, news story, or scandal occurs, how do you know if you should speak up? Speaking up can be scary, so you'll want to understand when it's appropriate.

How do you do that? Develop and publish belief statements. Belief statements are five to seven statements that describe who you are as an organization, what you believe, and why. They're also called value statements. Again, different terms mean the same thing. Organizations rarely craft these, but I wish they would do so more frequently because they help your staff and leadership be clear on what you believe.

Sometimes belief statements seem well ingrained in an organization, but they're not written down privately or publicly. Write them down! Here are some examples:

- We believe all children deserve parents.

- We believe it benefits everyone when adults with disabilities live and work in our community.

- We believe every animal deserves a second chance.

- We believe we must serve those who have served our country.

At *501creative*, we developed belief statements for Episcopal City Mission, a group that ministers to children in juvenile detention. We helped them develop these messages for their website so that people who aren't familiar with *why* kids are in jail will have empathy for them. Here are their belief statements:

- We believe that all children deserve a second chance.

- We believe in the healing promise of God's presence.

- We believe in providing a safe environment, free from judgment.

- We believe children aren't disposable and are worth our time and attention.

- We believe the children we serve are more than the worst thing they have done.

- We believe being there, providing a ministry of presence, is healing.

- We believe the calming presence of our chaplains reassures the children that someone cares about their spiritual well-being.

After reading these, do you feel more connected to this group? Do you have a greater understanding of what they do and why? No one can argue with an organization's beliefs. They are what they are. They are clear and concise statements about what's important and valued.

Work with your leadership to come up with your own, and then *live by them*. Be outspoken about them! This is critical to courageous communication. Why? If a public issue arises or a news story crops up—and you wonder if you should say something—then you have your belief statements to guide you.

Here's an example from Episcopal City Mission before they adopted belief statements. A child in juvenile custody in another state died, and reporters were looking for the local angle. Because Episcopal City Mission isn't responsible for caring for children, they declined the interviews. Later, after they adopted belief statements, they realized they could have said something like, "While our ministry is not responsible for the care of children in court custody, we believe our ministry has a calming and healing presence. We believe in the safety and well-being of every child. We think that having our chaplains with the children who are in custody has a calming and healthy presence and allows for a more positive atmosphere for children and staff."

You can't bore your audience into action. You can't ignore what is going on around you. You must take a stand and be courageous. Don't be afraid to communicate what you believe!

Beth Goad at Episcopal City Mission said it's so much easier to explain what they do and share the stories of children in court custody because of the messages we created but also because of the belief statements. It grounds and guides the organization as they move forward to be more courageous communicators. Next time a reporter calls, I know there will be a different response because they have the tools to communicate effectively.

> You can't bore your audience into action. You must take a stand and be courageous. Don't be afraid to communicate what you believe!

Before you start or jump into a public conversation, pause for a moment. Don't post, write, or tweet without answering these questions:

- Does the issue or story align with our mission and with our belief statements?

- Is the issue or story of value to our audiences?

- Would our participation in the issue or story add to the conversation?

If you can say yes to all three questions, then speak up. If not, don't.

Courageous communication doesn't mean you speak up about everything, all the time. It means you speak with a purpose: attracting like-minded people to your organization.

Consistency and Repetition

Strong communication means saying the same thing over and over and over again. It means maintaining a consistent look and message, which takes *discipline*. You know that your brand has value, and if you make a change, you need to weigh that change against the brand value.

I've been in discovery sessions where we were brainstorming a new name for a giving society, and someone wanted to change the tagline. That's not discipline. Find your message and stick with it. You think Target is going to say, "Hey, let's change this bull's-eye thing. It's boring."

"For every child, a place to call home" is the tagline of the Foster and Adoptive Care Coalition. It's everywhere, all the time, exactly the same. Maybe the staff is sick of it, but guess what? Even after almost ten years, we are still finding new audiences. We found something that works and we stuck with it.

For Further Thought

- What is your organization's brand promise?

- Trace the loyalty index for the last few consumer items you've purchased to understand how this tool works in your life.

- Determine where each of your audiences fit on the loyalty index.

- What are your organization's commonly held beliefs? Are they written down?

- How are you already exhibiting courageous communications? Where can you improve?

WHERE DID ALL THE DONORS GO?
How to Connect with Advocates and Find New People

'm going to blow your mind. Here goes: it's not your job to make people care about your nonprofit.
I KNOW!

It's not your job to make people care. It's your job to find like-minded people and convince them that your organization is the best choice for them.

How can this be? Because we reach people *emotionally* first. The formula is heart, then mind, then wallet. People won't give to or get involved with an organization that doesn't connect with them emotionally. And you can't *make* someone care. So don't worry about making people care. Find like-minded people and make it work for them.

> It's not your job to make people care. It's your job to find like-minded people and convince them that your organization is the best choice for them.

Codependent organizations want everyone to like and care about them, and that's not possible, practical, or realistic. We can't appeal to everyone.

No More "Spray and Pray"

We spend a lot of time, money, and mental energy trying to convince people that they should know who we are, and we're disappointed when they don't. I hear it all the time: no one has heard of us. OK—so? Who are these people? Do they need to know you? What happens after they know you?

Many years ago, the approach to marketing was "spray and pray": spread lots of messages and hope someone sees or hears and responds. It wasn't very efficient or effective, and it certainly wasn't measured. Who read that newsletter? What did our supporters need? Unless they told us, it was hard to know because we couldn't gauge their behaviors.

Today, we have many tools to connect with our supporters. We can see what emails they open and what they forward, read, share, and more. Now we can hone in on our best prospects.

Because of that, our approach needs to shift. We don't need to convince people of our worth. To convince everyone that your organization is worthy and valuable—only to have most of them decline to support you—is a waste of time, energy, and money.

Get Them to Come to You

The new approach is to find like-minded people and be available to them, so they're attracted to your organization. Get off the communication treadmill. Just stand still and be available and easy to find. This is called *inbound marketing*. Instead of going *outbound*, spreading your message and hoping someone responds, stand tall in your message and make yourself easy to find. Then when people who are interested in your cause go looking, there you are! And because they've self-identified as being interested, they already think you're worthy and valuable.

This approach means that you need to look at how you spend your money to see how well it's working. A local private school spent the largest portion of its marketing budget on advertising (outbound marketing—a "spray and pray" approach), when only 3 percent of families indicated that they had learned about the school from the ads. The most effective form of marketing was word of mouth from families, friends, and coworkers, the best example of inbound marketing. The school cut back on ads and encouraged its current families to share stories of the school.

It seems weird to stop chasing after prospects. It may feel like you're not doing your job. But when you focus on sharing stories of value and interest, and on being helpful, available, and accessible, people will respond. It gets you off the tread-mill and delivers results.

> When you focus on sharing stories of value and interest, and on being helpful, available, and accessible, people will respond. It gets you off the treadmill and delivers results.

Another way to attract people is to entertain them. Entertain or educate. Do one or the other. Make it less about what you want to say and more about fulfilling the needs of others.

We like to laugh—and cry. And yet, I think nonprofits are more scared of being silly and funny than they are of being controversial. But fun can touch people and make you memorable. What about your work makes you laugh? Show your faults, your falls, your disasters. Show your people having fun.

Everyone wants to "go viral," and that means your content must be authentic, honest, interesting, and different. You can't force something to capture mass attention, but if you show the heart of what you do and try to be as unfiltered as possible, you'll capture attention. Moving away from codependent communication to courageous communication is scary but worth it.

> You'll attract more supporters by taking risks than by staying safe.

Like my burlesque class, be whatever you want, but *don't be boring!* You'll attract more supporters by taking risks than by staying safe.

For Further Thought

- What outbound marketing strategies does your organization employ?

- What are your inbound strategies?

- Which is more effective—inbound or outbound?

LONG-TERM LOVE:
How to Create Allies Who Are with You Through Good and Bad

'**ve officiated five weddings.** Part of that responsibility is to help write and shape the ceremony, and I've written vows and helped couples write their vows. While I was doing that, it made me consider all the other vows we think about but don't write—between parents and kids, neighbors, friends, and, of course, between nonprofits and their donors. What if we made vows for all our relationships? It simply means that you state how you'll help and support one another.

Imagine if you and your donors stood together to pledge your devotion:

"I, *nonprofit*, promise to support you and to make sure that your gifts have an important role in our organization. I promise to acknowledge your devotion in the way that is important to you. I promise to be transparent, honest, and authentic during our successes, failures, needs, and challenges."

"I, *donor*, promise to support you, knowing that my gifts are helping to realize a mission close to my heart. I promise to be understanding in good times and bad, to stick with you through triumphs and crises. I promise to be as generous as I can be because I know that my gifts are needed."

Wouldn't it be great if we actually said these vows to each other? Well, we do—but maybe not so deliberately. The key to building long-term relationships is to find people who share our heart and who care about what our organization cares about.

We all want donors who will be with us for the long haul, donors who know our organization and trust us enough that when bad things happen—and they will—they stick with us. They not only support us, they also champion us to family, friends, and colleagues. They feel a deep personal connection that is not easy to break.

> We all want donors who will be with us for the long haul, donors who know our organization and trust it enough that when bad things happen— and they will—they stick with us.

How do we find and cultivate these people? How do we find donor long-term love?

First, let's review how to stand strong in your brand and message to allow people to find you. What does this look like?

In Saint Louis, we had something happen here that you may have heard of. It became a buzzword—Ferguson. That day in August 2014 changed our city in fundamental ways. One organization stepped up almost immediately. Arch City Defenders, only five years old in 2014, was outspoken and unwavering in its commitment to civil, criminal, and social justice. And guess what? It grew fast. People who were frustrated with our civil and criminal justice system had a place to go to help create change. They talked about the problems and offered a solution. Actually, they didn't *offer* a solution; they *created* a solution.

Arch City Defenders had the nerve to stand up for what was important. The leaders often faced criticism, but they were also praised.

Other organizations around Saint Louis had much the same mission, but they weren't as vocal. I met with one such organization that had the same passion as Arch City but didn't know how to express it. As a result, their brand suffered because the people who cared about social justice perceived them to be out of touch. But they actually weren't out of touch. They were doing great work but were struggling to communicate that work.

Strong messages invite people to join you.

Strong messages galvanize the supporters you have.

I can't say it enough!

Focus on the Benefits

When we speak out, we may focus on what we might lose rather than what we can gain. That's a natural and normal response. Our brains are hardwired to fear change. What if we lose a donor or a sponsor?

But what might we gain? Who will see or hear our messages and gravitate toward us? Perhaps we're compelled to call out an injustice or an issue, no matter what the cost, because it's the right thing to do. That's a strong message, too.

When the benefits outweigh the concerns, you'll move forward. If you can determine the benefits, then you'll change. Your concerns will still be there, but they won't hold you back. The essential thing is for your organization to commit to the benefits of courageous communications.

Here's an exercise: Brainstorm with your leadership team about the benefits of courageous communication. What goals can it help you reach? What need will it help you fulfill? Could courageous communication help you find donors, volunteers, program participants, or students? Recruit donors who understand and trust you, so you increase donor retention? Find qualified prospects more easily?

BENEFITS AND CONCERNS

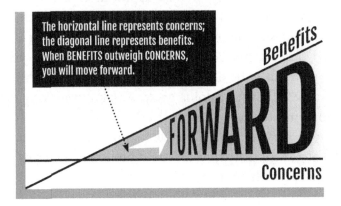

The horizontal line represents concerns; the diagonal line represents benefits. When BENEFITS outweigh CONCERNS, you will move forward.

Benefits

FORWARD

Concerns

Then list your concerns. This will be a lot easier to do, but list them anyway. Then make a plan to address those concerns.

I worked with an organization that wanted to change its name. At a board meeting, we listed all the benefits of the change, and then we listed the concerns. One by one, we went through each concern and made a plan to address them all. Concerns shouldn't keep us stuck. Just make a plan to address them.

Let Them See Right Through You

Being transparent is scary. It means that you let people see into your organization—the good and bad and everything in between. It means that you tell the truth, even if that truth is complicated or difficult. I've often heard nonprofit staffers and board members say, "It's a hard story to tell. It's complicated." That's OK. Trust your supporters to understand.

> Transparency is scary. It means that you let people see into your organization— the good and bad and everything in between.

Here are stories of two organizations that trusted themselves and their audiences and told the truth.

The first is the Scholarship Foundation. They provide scholarships for students who can't readily access higher education. To raise funds, they ran a beloved resale shop that carried only designer clothes. But the store wasn't making money. After long consideration, the leadership decided to close the store. The foundation's mission is to provide scholarships, and the store didn't help achieve that mission.

A loyal fan base of fashion-conscious women was very disappointed, but the foundation's staff and board stood firm in their decision. And they did a couple of things right. First of all, they empathized with their audiences. Karin McElwain-West, the external relations director, told them that she understood their disappointment. She loved the store, too! She didn't minimize the pain of the store's closing.

Second, she and Executive Director Faith Sandler explained their decision and the reasons behind it. They took the time to share the behind-the-scenes details, particularly the financial difficulties they'd encountered. She told the disappointed shoppers that they were stewards of this money, and the responsible course of action was to close the store.

You need to know that when you take a stand and you're saying something of interest, some people won't like it. In this case, it was a deliberate decision, and the staff and board had time to prepare for complaints and concerns. But they also sent a strong message to their donors:

- The foundation acts in the best interest of those we serve, even when it's hard.

- The foundation is a responsible steward of donors' gifts.

- We care enough about our supporters to take the time to address concerns and complaints and to welcome discussion of the situation.

This next story is about an organization in crisis:

Stray Rescue of Saint Louis, an organization that I've supported as a volunteer for twenty years, had a distemper outbreak in the fall of 2016. It spread through the shelter and made dozens of dogs sick. More than two dozen didn't survive. This was devastating to staff and supporters alike.

Every day, founder Randy Grim would go live on Facebook for about ten minutes and explain the events of each day, the health status of the dogs, and how they were being treated. He stammered and cried and was authentic in his distress. He wanted to be transparent because he knew that's what the supporters expected.

It wasn't an act. Randy has devoted his life to the rescue of city street dogs, and to lose them like this broke his heart. He would say, "I owe it to our supporters to be completely authentic. I owe it to you guys to tell the truth." He did this every day for about a week, and as they worked through the crisis, he reported every few days. He never backed down or hid from the situation. He didn't try to hide his fear or pain.

A lot has changed since then. Randy and his team did something amazing. They took that crisis and used it to improve the shelter, the organization as a whole, and their relationships with partners and supporters. Donations poured in. They overhauled the adoption system. They improved their intake procedures. And they shared all these stories.

The tragedy turned into long-term improvements and increased the love and trust of donors. I'm a sappy sort, and I like to think that those poor babies didn't die in vain. The crisis brought about changes that probably wouldn't have been instituted any other way.

Welcome Criticism

Bad things happen. Let's accept that. People criticize and judge. Let's accept that. It's how we manage those bad times and those criticisms that makes a difference. We can't avoid them. And if we do or say things that are interesting, somebody's not going to like it.

Oprah Winfrey became famous because she says and does interesting things. She's vulnerable. She doesn't hide her

> Bad things happen. Let's accept that. People criticize and judge. Let's accept that. It's how we manage those bad times and those criticisms that makes a difference.

insecurities. Some people love it; some don't. And that's OK. Just because someone doesn't like what we do doesn't mean we're doing it wrong.

Now you're probably thinking, *But that's Oprah! If we make someone mad, it could be really bad. Since we're a nonprofit, our risks are higher.*

But the risk of silence is way higher. The real risk is that people underestimate you or overlook you completely. Faith Sandler at the Scholarship Foundation and Randy Grim at Stray Rescue stood firm in the face of criticism, and their organizations survived. The cost of hiding from that would have been much, much higher. Donors and volunteers would have left in droves. Did they lose a few? Probably. But they gained so much more.

We're Horrible, and We Can't Wait to Tell You About It!

Failure. No one wants to admit it. We're bad with money, or food, or whatever. We screw up; we mess up. And we feel all alone because everyone else must have their act totally together, right?

They don't; no one does. Darn it, I wish it weren't true! But in cognitive behavioral therapy, you don't fix your issues; you try to accept that you'll always have issues.

Mind. Blown. Again!

I went to therapy to get "fixed." I want to be confident in myself, have way less FOMO (fear of missing out), trust more, be less dependent on what others think, etc. Guess what? Ain't gonna happen! My job is to understand that we all have stuff we're working on and to accept that I have flaws and always will. It's like Whack-A-Mole. Smack one issue or problem down, and up pops another.

When we admit our failures or weaknesses, and our losses, we become more human. Our honesty earns respect. We all have issues, and when we share them, we connect more deeply with others.

Your nonprofit is the same. To admit what's wrong and say where you failed is the bravest thing you can do. And by being brave, you'll get the attention you want and the loyalty you crave.

> To admit what's wrong and say where you failed is the bravest thing you can do. And by being brave, you'll get the attention you want and the loyalty you crave.

What if you produced an annual report about your failures? Engineers Without Borders in Canada did this, and it was really cool. It was different and bold, and I love them for it. Because what happens when we fail? We learn—and we do it better the next time. When we tell stories of our failures, we show our donors that we're always learning so we can do it better. That's a story worth sharing.

We learn and grow through failure. It's how we find out what's truly important. When you share stories of failure, you're sharing how you learned lessons that improved you or your organization.

Fail away, darlings!

For Further Thought

- When has your organization faced criticism? How did you respond?

- What are the benefits of communicating courageously?

- What are your concerns about being a courageous communicator?

- Find an example of a failure you could communicate. How do you think that would be received?

EMPTY TABLES, EMPTY CHAIRS:
How to Get Your Leadership Engaged Around Courageous Communication

'd been speaking at conferences and workshops for years, giving talks on how to improve a website or brand an organization. But over time, I sensed that this learning was frustrating for the participants because they went back to their offices with big ideas and new perspectives, only to fall flat because they'd been taught new ways of *doing* things, not new ways to *feel* or *think*. I'm certain they knew that courageous communication was the right thing to do. They wanted to be interesting and strong in their messaging, but something kept them from doing so.

Now my workshops focus on teaching people how to manage the feelings and change the thinking of the stakeholders who aren't in the room, namely, the higher-ups who run their institutions. I tell them that they already know how to communicate effectively but that the *codependent culture* prevents them from doing it.

As a general rule, nonprofit board members are somewhat risk averse. I get that. I'm on the board of an organization as well, and I know that we're responsible for the fiscal health of the organization. But given that, how do we change culture?

How can we see courageous communication not as a risk but as a benefit? And as a moral mandate? Sometimes we need to speak up, no matter the cost. How can we change the culture to say, "Hey, we know it's scary to be authentic, but it will benefit us in the long run." It's all about maximizing benefits and minimizing risks, with a healthy dose of patience.

> It's all about maximizing benefits and minimizing risks, with a healthy dose of patience.

I'm on the board of Foster and Adoptive Care Coalition, and our board is full of prominent corporate types who provide expertise and connections. They're fantastic people, no question. When I first introduced the concept of courageous communication to them, I listened to their concerns, and we addressed them, one by one. We talked about expanding our social media presence by commenting, sharing, retweeting, etc. I talked and talked about why it's so important to build a community of support. Finally, someone said, "Yeah, ummm, we don't know how to do any of that."

Now I understood. It wasn't that the board didn't want to support social media efforts. They didn't know how. We took a step back and trained them how to participate more fully on Facebook. Thank goodness someone spoke up, or the staff and I would have walked away thinking no one cared!

Best Practices

There are some established best practices that you can incorporate to be more courageous in your communications. They are minimize risk with a plan, exercise patience and start slowly, start small, host one-on-one meetings, understand what motivates each board member, and share success stories.

• *Minimize Risk with a Plan*

If you already have a communications or marketing plan, be sure to show how courageous communication will help reach your goals and objectives. If you don't have a plan, this is the perfect time to create one. Plans give us a sense of purpose and control. The act of developing one can relieve the fear and anxiety of implementing new strategies.

A communications plan—specifically, one that focuses on developing an organizational personality that attracts people to you—can help the higher-ups feel in control. Remember the loyalty index? Think about how to move people from being unaware to becoming raving fans by using your plan. The plan can relieve anxiety and increase buy-in of leadership.

> A communications plan— specifically, one that focuses on developing your organizational personality to attract people to you— can help the higher-ups feel in control.

When all the concerns have been inventoried, use your plan to address each one of them. When you reconvene at a subsequent meeting, the plan will show how the new approach helped reach the organization's goals. Leaders like data, so use your plan to show the numbers.

Better yet, get another board member to present the data. Peer-to-peer communication is always better than staff-to-board reporting. After that, let the stakeholders sit with it. It will probably take some time for them to absorb the new information and evaluate the new way of doing things. Let them watch the process work.

• *Exercise Patience and Start Slowly*

Make an effort to find one champion, perhaps the executive director or a board member. If you don't have a communications and marketing committee, form one. When everyone in that group is clear on the direction, then you can broaden your audience. What you don't want to do, despite all the excitement I'm sure you'll have after reading this book, is go in with guns blazing and try to make a big change. Change is scary, especially when it seems forced upon us. So chill. Let me assure you that no one's ever described me as chill and patient. I know exactly how hard this will be for you.

- *Start Small*

At Foster and Adoptive Care Coalition, we shared a story about Simone Biles, a gymnast on the U.S. team at the 2016 Olympics. She'd been adopted by her grandparents and, of course, that was a huge feel-good story, the type of story the Olympics likes to showcase. During one of her competitions, announcer Al Trautwig referred to her adoptive parents as her grandparents. When a woman tweeted Trautwig to say that he should call them her parents, he responded: "They may be her mom and dad, but they are NOT her parents." That comment fueled news stories about adoption, birth parents, drug use, and family dynamics—and it exploded on social media.

In response, the coalition shared a pertinent article, added some comments, and posted it on Facebook and Twitter—because it was a conversation! And we could add to it. People were talking about a topic that was part of our mission, and we needed to be part of that conversation. At the time, that was our most-shared post, and it received the most comments. We *engaged* with our audience, and they engaged with us.

You don't always need to control the conversation, but it's important to be a natural part of the conversations that are already happening. After that success, we built on it. And we've never stopped speaking out about our concerns.

- *Host One-On-One Meetings*

I highly recommend hosting individual one-on-one meetings with board members every year. Here's why: it's not about what that board member can do for you but what *you* can do for *them*. As with all your communications, approach each of your board members with the attitude, "How can I be of service to you today?"

This is one way that you, as staff, can help each board member feel more connected, involved, and appreciated. Be open to their concerns and validate them. Courageous communication can feel risky, and if you don't treat that as a valid fear, you'll have roadblocks to creating a cultural change. Let them work through their concerns.

I look forward to our annual summer meeting at Foster and Adoptive Care Coalition. When I first joined the board, I was somewhat intimidated by the corporate lawyers and accountant types. These meetings allowed me to share my concerns about the value I bring to the board and also to brainstorm how I could best help.

- *Understand What Motivates Each Board Member*

Just as I had to understand my value to the board, the other members need to as well. Each member has specific needs and motivations. A happy, productive board will be more inclined to embrace change and try new things. Happy, productive boards create a culture of openness that fosters courageous communication.

> A happy, productive board will be more inclined to make change and try new things. Happy, productive boards can create a culture of openness that fosters courageous communication.

After winning a significant amount of money in a lottery, a friend of mine was pursued by organizations asking for donations. As exciting as that was, managing that prize money was also a big responsibility. She was frustrated by organizations that approached her for monetary donations because she also wanted to give her time and ideas. It seemed they saw only her money, not her. Of course, some people might want to write a check and move on. But my friend didn't want to be known for her money. She wanted these organizations to get to know her and her needs and to recognize her for what she had to share as a person, not just a pocketbook. Now she works with organizations that value what she values—not just the cash, but her time and her talent as well.

We allow others to lead us only when we know they understand us and care about our needs. Always ask, "How can I be of service to you? How can I help you?" Rather than foster codependence, this approach helps alleviate it. When you can learn about other people, you can work together and have a mutually beneficial relationship.

Learn about other people's needs. That doesn't mean you have to act on those needs; it just means you need to understand them.

• *Share Success Stories*

When you (a staff person or board member of a nonprofit) witness courageous communication, call it out—to yourself, to your staff, to your board, and to your committees. When you see something, say something! By drawing attention to it and complimenting those who do it, you help create a cultural shift.

Remember that article about Simone Biles that Foster and Adoptive Care Coalition shared and commented on? Why was it so successful? People were *already in the conversation*, and we added to it. After that, the board recognized how effective courageous communication can be, and from then on, wholeheartedly supported our efforts.

For Further Thought

- Take a look at your current communications plan (or develop one). What can you do to make it more courageous?

- Who in your organization could be a champion to help with the culture change? Make a list of names, and schedule some time to talk to them.

- What do other organizations do to communicate courageously? Do some research and see if they're doing something that would also work for you.

CAN'T WE FIND SOMEONE TO DO THIS FOR FREE?
How to Measure the Value of Your Marketing Investment

or years, I've worked as the strategist and resident extrovert at *501creative*. Let me tell you how this lovely place
got started.

Karen Handelman, our president, worked in corporate
design in Chicago but longed to do more meaningful work.
She and her husband packed up and volunteered with Habitat
for Humanity for a year, during which time she discovered
two things:

- Pro bono work was unreliable and often wasn't in the
  best interest of the nonprofit. Karen watched Habitat
  offices struggle with donated work that, however
  well-intentioned, didn't meet their needs. But how do
  you ask for something different when it's free?

- She wanted to work with nonprofits and apply her
  design skills to organizations that are working to better
  the community.

Karen decided to open a design firm exclusively for non-profits. It would be the bridge between the high-end ad agencies with their high-dollar fees and free services. This agency would deliver excellent results for reasonable costs. Everyone told her it was a horrible idea. *Nonprofits don't have any money. You'll never make enough to survive.* She ignored those voices and founded *501creative.* That was 1995.

And she has remained true to the mission. We exclusively serve nonprofits and try to keep our fees as reasonable as possible, while knowing that making an investment is necessary if you want good work.

You often hear, "Can't we get someone to do this for free?" Everyone wants a magical intern or design firm to give them quality work they don't have to pay for. I'm not saying that everyone who does pro bono work is ineffective. But if you want to be a grown-up organization that's committed to moving its mission forward, you'll have to invest in quality communications and marketing work.

> If you want to be a grown-up organization that's committed to moving its mission forward, you'll have to invest in quality communications and marketing work.

I can see you nodding your head in agreement. Like exercise or diet, you probably know the right thing to do but don't know how to do it. How can you change your culture so marketing is considered a valuable investment?

SOAPBOX ALERT:
Bust the Overhead Myth

You are allowed, right now, to stop for a few minutes to watch Dan Pallotta's talk on nonprofits. Check out his TED talk, "What We Think About Charity Is Dead Wrong." Pallotta came up with the concept of the Overhead Myth, which states that the percentage of charity expenses that goes to administrative and fundraising costs—commonly referred to as *overhead*—should not be the primary measure of a charity's performance. It's the *results* that matter.

Nonprofits often don't invest in themselves because those costs are considered overhead. But having a low overhead isn't the way to value your organization. You want *impact*. How is the world better because you are in it? Who cares if you keep your overhead costs under 15 percent if you aren't changing lives?

If you've been selling your organization to donors based on overhead, STOP! Use the information in this book to find a better way. And if your leadership is reluctant to spend money on marketing if it increases overhead, then you need to educate them.

Nonprofits are so concerned with keeping overhead low that they lack the resources to work effectively. Because organizations are unable to work effectively, they bring in too little money to boost fundraising efforts, so they can raise more money. We need to break this cycle, which is due to our codependent efforts to keeping donors happy, regardless of our needs. When we do what's right for us, do good work, and show strong outcomes, no one will care what our overhead is.

Back to our regularly scheduled programming.

Understand the Competitive Landscape

Yes, you have competitors. And *competitor* is often a dirty word in the nonprofit world. To soften it, I often say, "other like organizations." And we all know there are other organizations that do much the same thing that donors could contribute to or participate in.

Here's how you handle that.

Make a list of organizations that are in your field. Some organizations have crowded marketplaces with lots of other like organizations. Others may not. Every industry is different, so understand who else is playing in your sandbox. You're looking for two things:

- What are others doing?

- How are you different or better than they are?

Again, here's an uncomfortable word—*better*. If saying you're different helps, that's OK. The issue is, what do you do that no one else does?

The issue is, what do you do that no one else does?

I volunteer for Stray Rescue of Saint Louis. There is also the Animal Protective Association, the Humane Society of Missouri, and many others. How are they different? All work in animal welfare, but they each approach the issue a little differently. Humane Society focuses on rescues and investigations, APA focuses on connecting humans with animals, and Stray Rescue focuses on abused and abandoned city street dogs. And along with their different missions, each organization has a different personality. If these organizations were people, Humane Society would be the grand dame: established, trustyworthy, experienced. APA is down-home and folksy, approachable, and relaxed. Stray Rescue represents the misfits. They are bold, often controversial. The upstarts.

To determine where your organization fits in the mix, ask yourself these questions:

- Who are your competitors?

- What do you do that is different or better?

- If your competitors were people, what would their personality be like?

- What would your organization's personality be like?

When *501creative* works with a client, we take a look at who else is out there. How can we position your organization to be different? How can we help people understand your specific position?

As a consumer, I should be able to look at your website and, within fifteen seconds, understand what makes you different or better. Understanding what makes your organization different or better than others also helps fuel your brand promise and your messages. It all works together.

If you can show your leadership that others are beating you at your game, it will help build your case for more investment in marketing and communications.

> As a consumer, I should be able to look at your website and, within fifteen seconds, understand what makes you different or better.

If the personality your nonprofit projects doesn't reflect who it really is, it's time to make some changes.

Make a Plan

We talked about plans in the last chapter, and they're one of the best tools you have to measure the effectiveness of your marketing and communications efforts. When you have goals and measurable objectives, you can show how your efforts are helping you reach your program or development goals. Make a plan, include your board and committees in the process, and use it. Don't put it on a shelf. Report on it to leadership regularly. In order to get the board to make an investment, you must show them the value of what you're already doing.

Conduct a Communications Assessment

Here's how it works. Gather everything you can find about your organization in print or online: your website, e-news, print news, brochures, display, video, promotional items—everything. Put them in a room with a few other people. Ask these questions for each item:

- Does the material visually represent your organization? Is there consistency in color, design, and layout? Does it all look like one family, and does that family accurately represent your organizational personality?

- Are the messages compelling and interesting, and do they move people to action? Do they tell your story? Do they represent your brand promise?

- How much time did it take to create each piece? Was it done in-house or with a vendor? How many hours of staff time did it take? How much money did the piece cost to make?

My personal opinion is that a lot of us spend too much time working on print newsletters or e-newsletters. It's a way to convince yourself that you're building relationships and fundraising, but you're really just writing a lot of copy that no one reads. An assessment can help you understand what you're doing that's most effective and what is not.

Free Isn't Free. Stop Looking for Pro Bono Work

Here's the thing: every once in a while, you come across a wonderful person or company that donates great things to your organization—a web developer, a marketing firm, or a photographer who provides quality work for free. This is like gambling and winning—nice when it happens, but don't bet on it every time.

Ask your board members a personal question: If they want something done around their house, do they try to get it for free? Do they automatically go with the lowest bid? Heck no! They know that quality, professional work costs money and that there are many variables to a partner or vendor relationship that have nothing to do with price. Use that same philosophy here.

Free is not sustainable or reliable. Marketing and communications efforts need to be consistent, focused, and sustained. You can't get that for free.

At *501creative*, we worked with many organizations over the years that got free stuff but found it wasn't worthwhile. It took so much effort that the staff could have either done it in house or paid for it.

> Free is not sustainable or reliable. Marketing and communications efforts need to be consistent, focused, and sustained. You can't get that for free.

Know the Real Cost of Your In-House Work

I have a particular point of view that's shared by other fundraisers I know. People frequently confuse *marketing* and *fundraising*. If I'm creating a print newsletter, then I must be relationship-building, right? While it's important to communicate with donors, indirect communication like print materials, e-newsletters, etc., should not be done at the expense of asking for money.

I know that the fear of asking for money is a pervasive—and valid—fear. And in the theory of codependent nonprofits, feelings are always valid. It's OK to be afraid to ask for money. But with the tools of courageous communication, you'll be able to speak to donors with a new clarity and confidence.

I think our communications folks spend too much time writing and producing materials when they could be building relationships that will sustain the organization. Let's take a look at the things we produce and why, and at what it actually costs to produce them.

An organization recently came to see us at *501creative* and asked us to revamp their newsletter. That sucker was sixteen pages with tons and tons of copy! It took their staff a long time to write, edit, and publish it. But they didn't know how long it took because those hours weren't tracked. Further, it was mailed out to about five thousand people, and most of them weren't donors. What's the point of putting in hours and hours of work to reach people who may or may not care? And with print, there's no way to know who's reading it.

So they pared the newsletter and their mailing list, and found an outside designer to produce the materials, which gave their staff thirty additional hours each month for the critical work of fundraising and event management. It now costs the nonprofit less, is a better product, and goes to donors who actually support the organization. Win, win, win!

Word of Mouth Is Beautifully, Blessedly Free

Encourage your allies to share your story with their own personal spin. Your allies are your strongest asset. Your staff are paid to say good things, and when someone voluntarily shares your message, it means something.

If you are noticeable and interesting, people will talk. Of course, all of them won't say good things. But if you say something important, have the courage to

> If you say something important, have the courage to have conversations that matter, and manage your praise and criticism, you're going to get attention.

have conversations that matter, and manage your praise and criticism, you're going to get attention.

I have a friend who used to volunteer for an organization that promotes reading to kids in schools. Every time she went to a school to read, she posted about it on Facebook. Here's what I love about this:

- She did this because she was committed. I could feel her passion.

- It didn't feel forced because she was a volunteer, not paid staff.

- I got to see the different schools and settings, which showed me the depth and breadth of what the organization does.

Do you invite people to share their stories? Stories are not only free; they're the most compelling way we can share our messages.

For Further Thought

- List all like organizations in your competitive landscape. Discover what you do that's different or better.

- Describe your organizational personality.

- How do your communications materials reflect that personality?

GETTING TO KNOW YOU:
Learn What Your Audiences Need and Want

"**Now here's something** we hope you'll really like!" That was a hallmark of the *Rocky and Bullwinkle* cartoons of my youth. And this is our intent for all we do for our audiences. We hope we're producing content and materials that they'll REALLY LIKE!

How do you know what your audiences need and want?

Understanding your audiences isn't a one-time thing. It's an ongoing process. Putting systems in place to gather opinions and build relationships is a sustained effort. Without bowing too much to our codependence, we need to know what our donors are thinking and feeling, in order to meet their needs. Remember, the goal is to create a mutually beneficial relationship that works for the organization and its audiences, whether it's volunteers, donors, program participants, board, staff, or anyone else.

> The goal is to create a mutually beneficial relationship that works for the organization and its audiences, whether it's volunteers, donors, program participants, board, staff, or anyone else.

Discovery Sessions

One of the most powerful tools I use to understand audiences is a discovery session. Discovery sessions happen at the beginning, long before any major decision-making takes place. I use these sessions for communication purposes, and there are two different models: a bridge and a path.

For messaging, I use a visual of two islands connected by a bridge. The bridge symbolizes our communication strategies, because what we're really doing is building a bridge so people can move closer to us. The bridge metaphor makes *communication* seem less ominous and unwieldy. We're simply building a bridge.

The second visual is a path. I use this when we're looking at specific communications to recruit people—students, volunteers, whomever. It's a path that has some roadblocks and barriers we need to overcome to gain participation.

Here's why discovery sessions are important:

- They provide input before any action is taken, which builds trust for when you make decisions later on.

- The structure allows different voices to be represented in an egalitarian way.

- The participants are invested in whatever you produce later. When people are included in the process, they're more likely to help maintain the brand. If they're involved in crafting the solutions, of course they'll be more likely to adopt those solutions.

- It's a great way to educate your group about the importance of branding and marketing.

I love these sessions. I've been doing them for years, and they always produce results.

Here's how they work. First, every participant writes down the answers to these three questions:

- What three words describe our organization?
- What two things make us different or better than other like organizations?
- Why do you think our audiences love us?

Next, we read our answers to each other and discuss them. It's important that everyone write out their answers before the discussion begins because writing gets to the heart of things, to the honest opinions. For one thing, if you're the only one in the room who thinks a certain way, you may hold back your opinion. Using this method, everyone gets a voice. And since some folks won't talk in a large group, this is a way to get everyone to participate. Finally, you'll have a written record of the conversation as it happens, which cuts down on note-taking.

I once worked with an organization called Girls in the Know, which provides sexual and adolescent development education to girls. We wanted to improve their messaging. Their tagline, *Knowledge is Power*, was OK but not great. It wasn't really their lead issue. At the discovery session, we explored the words that described the organization and realized that *knowledge* said a lot more than simply *power*. Their message was actually about connection, love, safety, and confidence.

So we extended the tagline into a campaign and rotated through those words. The word *knowledge* begins each phrase, and the last phrase ends with *knowledge is power*.

Knowledge is safety
Knowledge is confidence
Knowledge is connection
Girls in the Know: Knowledge is power

We took a so-so tagline and made it stronger to beef up their messaging. All this came through our discovery session, which took only a few hours. Now the staff and board are enthusiastic about their messaging because they helped create it.

Focus Groups

Focus groups differ from discovery sessions because they either test out a specific idea or solve a specific problem. A focus group is a set of like people who have a common role in the organization, whereas a discovery session is comprised of a cross-section of people.

I wish all organizations took the time to assemble ten to twelve people to get their input. It's not expensive to run a focus group, plus people love to give their opinions and you get lots of solid feedback. You also strengthen relationships with everyone in the room.

A few years back, *501creative*'s friends at Big Brothers and Big Sisters of Eastern Missouri were given a national campaign to use that was handed down from the national level. The theme was "Start Something," but Executive Director Becky Hatter thought we could do better. I'll admit I was a little intimidated by this project. After all, what new could we say about such a well-known organization?

We decided to host a series of separate focus groups with their board, the staff, the big brothers and big sisters (the "Bigs"), and the little brothers and little sisters (the "Littles"), along with their parents. We asked why Bigs get involved, why Littles get involved, what the connection means, and for ideas to recruit more of them.

By far the most chaotic focus group of my entire life was with those Littles. Maybe it was the pizza, soda, and candy we gave them, or maybe it was that they were sitting in a room after they'd sat in school all day, but they were *off the wall!* We did, however, get some good information from them.

After meeting with all four groups, it was clear that the value system at BBBS was about *long-term relationships.* In fact, if the match between a Big and a Little lasted less than a year, it hurt a child. For the program to work, the relationship needed to span several years.

Now I knew why "Start Something" didn't resonate. They didn't want to start something. The goal was to develop long-term relationships. We came up with the slogan "Be There, for Good." The *good* could mean for a long time, or for the good of the community, or for the good of the individual. Then we took it a little further: be there for ice cream, be there for graduation, be there for good.

To their credit, they took this concept, embraced it, and made it a part of the fabric of the organization. I knew it was hit when I was raking leaves in my yard and listening to Missouri Tigers football on the radio. A commercial for a local pretzel shop that gave a percentage of sales to BBBS came on and said, "Be there for pretzels!" I dropped my rake and did a happy dance!

That's what branding is about: you take your message and make it a part of everything you do. That message worked because it resonated with the organization, and it resonated because we did the research to uncover their true values.

Learn to Manage Criticism

Most of us don't ask for feedback because we're afraid we'll hear something horrible: this event was awful, you can't do your job, you're incompetent. This kind of criticism drives straight to the heart of our insecurities. And as good codependents, we give these negative voices far too much credence because they match our own internal insecurities. They validate our negative thinking.

I hate criticism. I remember every negative thing that anyone has ever said to me. It sits in this ugly spot in my brain that I go to when I'm feeling bad about myself, usually very late at night. I read evaluations with one eye closed, ready to slam the other one shut at the first negative word. I'm with you that criticism hurts. But if we're going say anything interesting, we have to know that everyone won't like it. And that's OK.

Criticism hurts. This world can be cruel. Just read the comments section for any online story, and you want to roll up into a ball and hide forever because people can be mean. So how can we deal with criticism?

First, accept it. If you say or do anything interesting, worthwhile, or different, *someone* isn't going to like it. Before social media, people could say bad stuff and we wouldn't know it. But now we do! And this fear of criticism can paralyze us. We have to accept that it will be there.

> If you say or do anything interesting, worthwhile, or different, *someone* isn't going to like it.

Second, create a policy. Your social media policy should outline how to deal with negative feedback. Here's a hint: don't delete it; deal with it! It's OK for people to have opinions, and we can decide as an organization if we want to respond to them.

Most people want to be heard and validated. Just because someone thought the band was too loud at your last event, it doesn't mean you turn the music down next year. It means you validate the comment ("Sorry they were so loud!") and offer a suggestion ("Let's seat you closer to the back next year, so you can enjoy the music without it being too loud.")

Back when social media was young, nonprofits were terrified of being on Facebook because, OMG, what if someone made a negative comment? So what if there was a negative comment? Will the world stop turning? Will your organization fall apart? Probably not. Address the comment if you want to, and move on. Know that criticism means you are heard and you are comment-worthy.

A friend once told me about how her executive director behaved after a big event. The attendees had filled out comment forms, and he pored over every one of them. He laser focused on each and every issue—like the music and the food—and literally obsessed over it. I was like, "Whoa! That's codependence right there!"

Beating yourself up about a few negative comments after a very successful evening is the definition of codependence. The executive director wanted to change the event based on this feedback, but my friend held strong. They decided that she'd reach out to everyone who made a negative comment to let them know they'd been heard, then let it go after that.

There are more avenues than ever for people to express their opinions. But you get to decide what to do with that feedback, and you can decide—as an organization—if there's anything you want to change.

For Further Thought

- How has your organization managed criticism in the past?

- When have you been reluctant to share your message because you wanted to avoid criticism? Who or what were you afraid of?

- Name some examples of when your organization was courageous after receiving a criticism.

SOCIAL MEDIA IS SCARY!
How to Manage Risk in the Online Wild West

I 've fostered a lot of puppies, and I know what a chore it can be to raise one. The Animal Protective Association of Missouri knows, too, and they did some courageous communications around that. They developed a social media campaign they called "Grown Ass Adult," which heralded the benefits of adopting adult dogs: they know the furniture isn't a fire hydrant, you don't have to come home from work for a midday potty break, etc. On National Puppy Day, they hosted a Grown Ass Adult Happy Hour with local beer, a signature cocktail, and grown ass adult (human) food—with half-price adoptions for adult dogs and cats.

This campaign was a rousing hit because it entertained *and* educated. "Adopt An Adult Dog" is not nearly as memorable. Yes, they used the word *ass*, and I would have loved to have heard the discussions surrounding that. They took a risk, and it paid off!

That doesn't mean you have to use questionable language in your campaigns. It means you need to take risks to get attention. I'm sure they got a few complaints, but I think the

APA knows its image and its audience, and it marketed to them. When we get past our fears, great things can happen.

Social media can be a scary place, especially for our sweet, wonderful nonprofit organizations. It feels like being thrown in with the mean girls in high school who are overly important and overly critical. We read the comments to stories and think, "How can we ever play in these spaces? These people are horrible!" Our codependence and fear of criticism are so great that we don't think we can handle the scrutiny of the wild online world of social media. Or, we play in such a small, limited way—being careful to stay safe—that we make no impression at all.

But it's more than the trolls and negative comments. Social media feels scary because it smashes the constructed hierarchy of what we share, to whom, and how. Our polished images, proofed press releases, and carefully crafted statements are broken wide open, and everyone and anyone is allowed to comment. With social media, everyone has power because everyone has a voice.

> With social media, everyone has power because everyone has a voice.

My aim is to convince you that when everyone has a voice, it's a good thing. It can help you retain supporters, find new ones, and create communities of support for your organization.

As I write this book, my beloved Stray Rescue of Saint Louis is named in two lawsuits brought by past employees who allege racial discrimination, sex discrimination, and mistreatment of animals. Because I'm a longtime and vocal supporter of Stray Rescue, many people have asked me how I feel about this. I've also paid close attention to the comments on social media and the comments below the online news stories.

First, because I'm a longtime supporter, the controversy hasn't changed much for me. And I've noticed from the comments that the same is true for others. If they've had a positive experience with Stray Rescue, they don't think the lawsuits have merit, and the consensus is that these are disgruntled employees. But if they've had a negative experience with the organization, they think the lawsuits have merit and are exposing issues within the organization. The bottom line is that the controversy hasn't changed anyone's mind. It's simply galvanized current supporters and confirmed the beliefs of former supporters.

Why is this important? Because it's hard to do *anything* without someone commenting on it, but those comments rarely change minds. We've never been more exposed to criticism—in both our personal and professional lives—and it's daunting. If we don't know how to handle criticism, we tend to stall in fear, and our codependence prevents us from communicating our needs, triumphs, failures, joys, and passions.

> If we don't know how to handle criticism, we tend to stall in fear, and our codependence prevents us from communicating our needs, triumphs, failures, joys, and passions.

Here's what you need to know—and it's in **bold** letters—so pay attention:

The risk of *not* becoming more social is too great to let fear control what you communicate.

Our future donors, supporters, volunteers, and program participants are active on social media in one form or another. This channel of communication isn't going away, no matter how much you ignore it or wish it would. You need to play in these spaces and be a part of these conversations.

Communications decisions should be made with rational thought, not with a dysfunctional fear that if we say, do, or respond to something, the organization will come apart at the seams.

In behavior change psychology, when the benefits outweigh the concerns, you will move forward. Think about that. The concerns don't go away, but if you can find the benefits, you'll have the courage to push through those concerns. THIS IS HUGE because many times we have no idea why we need to be on Facebook or Snapchat or Instagram or anything else. It's one more thing in the to-do pile.

Steps for Being Social

When you attach the benefits—meaning that you understand how social media will help you achieve your program or fundraising goals—you can see its value. Once you see the value, you're more likely to move forward. Here's how to do that.

Identify Your Fears

Concerns are always valid. If you know social media and roll your eyes at the stodgy higher-ups that poo-poo all this hashtag stuff, listen to them. Their complaints are simply a fear of the unknown. Remember, they get to have their feelings.

Feelings are fine, and it's good to express them, but we don't make decisions based on feelings; we make decisions based on rational thought. If the feelings or concerns aren't addressed, you'll be stuck in the fear of those who are afraid of new—or not so new—communication.

When I work with groups on communicating more courageously, we inventory our concerns and make a plan to address them. This is for social media as well as any other change or new approach. This may come across as skepticism, but it is really fear. These people will fight the whole process and may even sabotage it if they feel their concerns aren't addressed.

Create a Social Media Plan

Plans make people happy. They give things that seem out of control a sense of purpose. I bet that most of you who are reading this don't have a social media plan. There are as many plans as organizations. They don't have to be long or elaborate, but they do need to address a few things:

- **Goals and objectives:** How will social media help you meet your program or fundraising goals? How will you know when you've achieved those goals? Remember, when benefits outweigh the concerns, you're going somewhere! Find the benefits.

- **Audiences:** Who are your audiences, and where do they spend time on social media? Every year the Pew Research Center puts out a social media fact sheet that shows who's using what and for how long. It's comprehensive and easy to understand and can help you manage the concerns of skeptics.

- **Strategies:** These address which social media platforms you'll use, what content you'll provide, and who's responsible for getting it done and in what timeframe.

- **Editorial calendars:** An editorial calendar outlines what to post and when, yet it shouldn't be so rigid that you can't address issues as they arise. A calendar can give structure to what you want to say and when, but you'll want to follow the ebb and flow of the conversation and be able to shift with the drift. If you have something really important to say, make sure it gets discussed, but not at the expense of other conversations.

SOAPBOX ALERT:

Everyone is on the social media team. Don't think it's only the responsibility of the marketing or communications person. You're creating communities of support, and the more people who comment, share, and participate in that community, the stronger it will be. You need to create cultures that support social media participation.

I know this seems scary, because what if an employee says something awful? OK, what if? You can create policies to address that. If you want to create community, you need high levels of participation from all your constituents. This is possible if you remember that everyone is on the team. It can't be about one person.

What if you went to a party and only one person was allowed to speak? That's not relationship-building; that's grandstanding. Get everyone on board, and start building relationships.

Stepping off my soapbox now . . .

Create a Social Media Policy

Policies, like plans, relieve anxiety because they give us some guidance and help us understand what's OK and what's not. If I were writing a policy, it would be, "Don't be a jerk" or "If you wouldn't say it to your mom or boss, don't say it online." But most organizations want more detail than that. Yet that's really the essence of a social media policy.

If people are afraid to post, you lose all that passion and energy of your staff, volunteers, supporters, and participants. Give them power and trust.

My friend works for a bank, and he can't post on social media—even personally—about politics. He agreed to this (that would be very hard for me!) and understands the restriction. While that may seem extreme, it's their policy, and he adheres to it. You can make your policy say anything you want, but try to keep it as open as possible. Here are some things I *don't* want to see in a policy:

- **Don't require your people to post:** My nephew sells cars and at one dealership, he's required to make one Facebook post a day. That's not how we build relationships offline. Would you call someone every day, even if you had nothing to say?

- **Don't be required to have a dual personality:** The days are long gone when we had two Facebook accounts—one for work and one for our personal life. The personal *is* professional. We are in the business of relationship-building. Let your authenticity shine.

- **Don't deliver policy without training:** When you train everyone, you help them understand how social media supports the mission, how their participation can boost the organization, and how to engage with different social media platforms.

- **Don't forbid negative comments or criticism:** This is my biggie. Managing the criticism is key. Create a policy on how to address negative criticism. (The answer is not to delete the comment!) Criticism is a part of doing business, but it doesn't dictate your business. You can hear both praise and criticism, and decide how to respond. You don't have to act on either.

Kiss Control Goodbye

You can try to control your message, but it won't resonate in the social media space. Social media values authenticity, transparency, honesty, and responsiveness—not carefully crafted, heavily edited, and super-boring messages.

Create a plan and policy. Host trainings. Make sure your people have the tools to tell the story and the messaging to tell it well. And then trust them! You must let go of control and let things happen. The less control you need as an organization, the more your brand will flourish. Why? Strong brands have engaged supporters who feel ownership. They feel a personal connection. That's the key to having supporters with you through good and bad. The kind of people who know bad things happen and will still remain loyal. These are folks who have a personal connection and feel the pride of ownership with the organization. That's the most valuable supporter you can have.

Dive In

News has a cycle. A tweet lasts a few hours, a Facebook post a few more. Whatever you say, chances are, it will be forgotten soon enough. There isn't anything to do but do it!

Create or encourage a culture that's OK with experimenting and failing. Do what you can to relieve the fear of a policy, a plan, training, and messaging. And then go for it!

For Further Thought

- What's in your social media plan or social media policy?

- How do you currently handle negative comments on social media?

- Do you have supporters who became more engaged after a crisis? If you lost supporters, how did you handle it?

WE WANT ATTENTION, BUT DON'T MAKE US STAND OUT!
How to Find the Courage to Communicate Your Nonprofit's Authentic Personality

was standing in the mirror, loving my outfit. Tonight was my husband's holiday work party. For many years, he'd worked for a large corporation, but he'd recently moved to a biotech start-up. I admired my Santa-print dress and thigh-high, bright red, platform patent leather boots. I loved the look, but I was also a little worried. Would it be too much? After all, we were going to a work function. But then I thought, "Screw it! I love these boots, and if I don't wear them, I'm gonna be mad!"

When we walked into the party, one of my husband's coworkers and her friend were dressed like elves. My first thought was, "I'm so glad I wore these boots!" My second was, "I found my tribe!" I wasn't the craziest one at the party after all. The moral of this story is this: always be unapologetically yourself!

Your nonprofit organization can learn this lesson, too. When you communicate through your authentic personality, people feel connected and are drawn to you.

When you're authentic, you're interesting and entertaining, and you don't even have to try. Just like with burlesque dancing, you need to be interesting and entertaining, and you can do that only when you show your true personality.

How do you do that?

Marketing As an Exchange

All marketing is an exchange. With consumer goods, we exchange cash for items. I have money, and I want shoes. I give the shoe store money, and I get shoes.

Did you know that nonprofit fundraising is also an exchange? An organization helps families, provides mental health services, or rescues animals, which means that we—the donors—don't have to do those things. Donors give money so that nonprofits can create the change that donors want to see. That's an exchange, and it's an even one. We don't need to feel "less than" because we need money. We're helping our donors express their philanthropic needs.

My mentor, Carol Weisman, is one of the smartest consultants I know. (I want to be her when I grow up!) She stresses that fundraisers and nonprofit marketers exist to help people—donors—fulfill their philanthropic missions. That's how we serve them. There's an exchange that takes place between us, and it's an even one, which makes us as important as our donors. We don't need to put our donors' needs ahead of ours because their needs and our needs are equally important in the relationship.

We have a stake in the relationship, we matter, and we are just as important as our donors. Once we see the even exchange, we can let go of our codependence.

Push Marketing vs. Pull Marketing

Remember "spray and pray?" In the years before social media, nonprofits sent out newsletters and always included a response envelope for donations. We wouldn't dare send out a letter without asking for money; direct mail was too costly to pass up an opportunity to receive. We didn't even know who read that newsletter and who didn't. We just wanted to reach as many people as possible. We were *pushing out* information and hoping that someone would respond.

Since then, the world of communications has changed dramatically. Instead of buying attention and pushing messages out, we *pull* people toward us. This is called *pull marketing*, and it's an altogether different way of communicating.

Pull marketing doesn't try to convince people that your organization is worthy. Your job is to attract like-minded people to your organization. You can't control what's in the hearts of donors. In fact, their personal philanthropic wheelhouses are pretty much already set.

But things happen, and people can change their loyalties to nonprofits. My friend Rachel D'Souza Siebert, a fantastic fundraising consultant, had a heart attack shortly after her first child was born. Now she serves as a heart disease–prevention advocate. Her heart attack changed what was in her personal philanthropic heart, and because I support Rachel, I now support her fundraising efforts. Rachel is my primary reason for supporting her charities. It's not that I don't believe in heart health; it's just that it's not naturally in my philanthropic wheelhouse.

It's not worth your time or money to try to change what's in people's minds and hearts. Let go of the idea of push marketing. Push marketing means you're buying people's attention. Advertising, billboards, and commercials are all examples of push marketing.

Pull marketing means you earn attention by giving something of value. Pull marketing means the posts and the information you share with your supporters or future supporters are designed to interest them. In other words, it is not about *you*, it is about *them*; and when you make it about *them*, they'll be more interested in *you*.

PUSH VS. PULL MARKETING

The more honest and authentic you are in your communications, the more you'll attract like-minded people. And it takes courage to be honest and authentic, which means you have to tell the truth, even when it hurts.

Carol, my mentor, told me a great story. She was working with a research lab in Africa, helping them raise money. One of their donors was a wealthy Japanese investor. Oddly enough—and quite unfortunately—wild monkeys destroyed their lab. Like *for real!* Hundreds of thousands of dollars of damage was done. The researcher had been scheduled to Skype the donor, but now he wanted to cancel the call. How could he tell his investor that the lab had been destroyed?

"No," Carol told the researcher. "You always, always must be honest."

After that, the researcher made the call and told the truth. The donor immediately supplied the funds to repair and rebuild the lab, and the two cemented a relationship that culminated in the investor flying thirty members of his own family there for the researcher's wedding.

If you want to get attention, you have to say something interesting, and sometimes being interesting means mustering up the courage to have difficult conversations. You can't always play it safe in your messaging. You must have the courage to let go.

Here's another story: Ryan Farmer is the marketing guy for the Saint Louis Area Food Bank. This organization struggles with the fact that people love to donate food, but food drives don't do much to solve the issue of hunger. The truth is that food banks can do much more with money than with donated food. They have tremendous buying power and can get fresher, more nutritious food to those who need it. I mean let's face it—we often clean out our cabinets and donate that food, so it's not top-shelf stuff. Further, when people donate food, the food bank has to pick it up, inventory it, and check the expiration dates, etc. It's inefficient and expensive.

Should they be honest and say, "Listen, we appreciate the help, but we can do much more with money," or should they continue to participate in food drives?

According to the principles of courageous communication, *they have to tell the truth!* But it doesn't have to be an all-or-nothing truth. Slowly and over time, they can move away from food drives and seek monetary donations. For the Saint Louis Area Food Bank, it means developing strong messaging—maybe even a campaign—around this idea. A virtual food drive or a bin-removal campaign can bring some fun to the idea as well. The point is to trust the audience to understand. And if some people still need to have those cans in their hands, they probably weren't going to donate money anyway.

People might be critical of a food bank that doesn't collect food, but that's no reason to continue a practice that's not working. You must do right by those you serve and those who give.

Inventory Concerns

Remember benefits and concerns? When the benefits outweigh the concerns, you'll move forward. But concerns will always be there. It helps to list them and develop ways to address each one.

I worked with the board of an organization that had a horrible acronym for their name. It was awkward, hard to remember, and boring. The board wanted to change the name, but they had concerns.

In a group session, we listed all the benefits of a name change: it would be easier to find new program participants; it would be easier for people to understand the mission; it would be easier to remember the new name because it would reflect the organization's purpose and personality.

Then we listed concerns—every one of them. The board was afraid that alumni of this program would be confused and possibly wouldn't support the organization if the name were different. They were concerned that their current audiences wouldn't know that they were the same group with a new name. Then there were the costs associated with a name change for materials, signage, etc.

These were all valid concerns. We can't dismiss concerns because, as you know, concerns don't just disappear. Instead, we made a plan to address each of them. How could we keep alumni in the loop or, better yet, use the name change as an opportunity to engage this group? How could we help our current audiences understand that the only thing that changed was the name? One by one, we listed each solution on a white board.

The board finally understood that a name change could build their brand equity, and we made a plan to make the change more comfortable.

We Aren't Fortune-Tellers

Our feelings are just feelings; they don't predict the future. We might think it's all going to go wrong, but that doesn't mean it will. We strive to make decisions with rational thought, understanding the benefits and concerns, rather than in fear. We can't afford to live in fear.

The biggest roadblock to being courageous is we think we'll lose donors if we tell the truth or if we advocate for our cause. But is that true? First, we can't predict the future. Second, if we list our concerns or what we think the concerns of our donors will be, we can make a plan to address those. Third, we can also identify the donors we think will need the most attention or support and reach out to them. And if they leave, maybe they weren't that loyal to us anyway. Plus, we just might gain new donors who are excited about our message, mission, and commitment.

When we let go of fear, we find the courage to stand out in a way that's authentic to our organization, engages and excites our audiences, and is honest and loving to those we serve. One thing is certain: we won't bore anyone into getting excited about our organization.

> When we let go of fear, we find the courage to stand out in a way that's authentic to our organization, engages and excites our audiences, and is honest and loving to those we serve.

For Further Thought

- In what ways is your organization fearful?

- If marketing is an exchange, what do you offer your supporters?

I HAVE NO IDEA WHAT I'M DOING:
How to Create Staff Expertise

landed my first nonprofit job because I said, "yes" to one question. My future boss pointed to a Mac Classic computer and asked, "Can you work this machine?" That was 1992.

Desktop publishing, as we called it back then, was all the rage. I was part of the first generation of nondesigners who had design software at their fingertips. I worked for a social service agency for troubled youth and managed their publications, communications, and some events. I did it all on that Mac. Since my boss had no idea how to work that thing, I got the job. (Now I can imagine that many young people get jobs when a higher-up points to Facebook or Hootsuite and asks, "Do you know how to work this thing?")

Back then, I was young and inexperienced, but hungry. I worked hard to produce newsletters. Were they the most professional? Probably not, but I did my best.

Many people come into a nonprofit job in a similar way. They try to tackle code or software they know little about. They spend endless hours trying to update a website or write articles or lay out a newsletter. But is this the best use of employees' time and talents? Is this the way to communicate effectively?

You must make a decision. What's the best use of your expertise, and how can you best benefit your organization and its supporters?

Assess, Assess, Assess

I seem to say this a lot, but a communications assessment is the best way to find out what works and what doesn't. During the assessment, you want to ask, "Is this activity building relationships? Is this time better spent on other projects?"

In the next chapter, we'll talk more about *how we value our time*, but for now, I'm just going to say that *we don't*, and we should. When we finally understand the true costs of our internal project, valued by time and cost, we see how much our marketing efforts actually cost us.

Focus on Building Relationships

Your relationships are yours. They belong to you! These are your personal connections built over time and with great effort and patience. You can't hire people to step in and conduct your relationships. You can—and should—hire people to develop web content, create newsletters, or build or maintain a website, but there are no substitutes for building and maintaining your relationships.

Here's the big message: when you spend time away from relationship building, you leave money on the table. When other things take you away from building relationships, you have less time to spend with your donors, who are your biggest source of income. According to Charity Navigator, 72 percent of all giving comes from individuals. You must make their care and feeding your priority. You must continually tell them your story.

My smartest branding clients host trainings to help them develop their messaging and talking points. I have brought people to tears—yes, actual tears!—by helping them tell their story clearly, in a brief and compellingly manner.

Hire Out the High-Expertise Work

If what you're doing isn't about relationship-building or requires a high level of expertise—like graphic design, coding, or video production—hire the experts. Here's why: it will take too long for your staff to develop a level of competency, and the outcome most likely won't be that good. I can just hear you say, "Hey, we'll build that website in house to save money!" But here's the rub: it's going to take someone hours and hours to learn a skill that won't be needed again. Keep the staff focused on marketing tasks that build relationships and generate income.

> Keep the staff focused on marketing tasks that build relationships and generate income.

Yes, it costs to take projects out of house, but a focused staff will generate more revenue, and that, in the long run, will make you more money.

Hire Short-Term Expertise

Personal trainers help us get fit; therapists help us understand and manage our feelings, thoughts, and behaviors; financial planners help us save and spend effectively. We go to experts for guidance.

Nonprofit consultants like me can do the same for your organization. We can offer a big-picture perspective. I wish more organizations would consider getting a third-party view of their activities. It doesn't have to be a big expense, but it can save you time and money because it helps you to be more effective.

One organization shared their story with me:

"We felt like we were doing the right thing, but we weren't sure. For a long time, we didn't think we could afford to hire a consultant, but we decided to spend two hours a month with one to help us assess our big picture. Now we know we're on track; and when issues come up, we have an economical way to manage them."

Let It Go

Many of us have a "pile on" approach to our work. We add new things to the to-do pile without figuring out what we don't need to do anymore. This leaves us overworked and not as effective as we could be.

If something isn't working, let it go. We made the decision at *501creative* not to produce an e-newsletter. It wasn't an easy decision because we felt like we were somehow cheating, like we weren't doing things "right." But here's the thing: we hadn't issued them frequently enough, we were horrible at list maintenance, and an email newsletter didn't generate clients. So we stopped. And guess what? We survived!

Remember how we worked with a private school that spent most of its marketing budget on advertising? They surveyed their current families and learned something awesome: most people learned about the school via word of mouth. Happy parents told other parents. They stopped most of the ad buys and used that money to create tools for current parents to share their story. Once they

Bottom line: Use your staff to build relationships, and hire experts for everything else.

understood what was effective and what wasn't, they were able to let go.

Bottom line: Use your staff to build relationships and hire experts for everything else.

For Further Thought

- What percentage of your staff duties build relationships?

- What percentage of staff duties do not directly build relationships?

- What could you hire vendors or consultants to do to increase your staff's ability to build relationships?

TIME *IS* ON MY SIDE:
How to Use Time More Effectively to Get Better Results

You've heard the phrase "time is money," but how many of us really live it? I feel guilty if I spend money on something I could do myself, like cleaning the house, washing the car, or cooking dinner. I should be doing those things, not paying someone else to do them. And yet, my time is valuable. The question is, are these activities the best use of my time?

I think women, in particular, struggle with this. We feel guilty when we make our lives easier because we assume it's at the expense of others. It took me a while to learn where to allocate my time and energy. Paying others to help me meant I could write a book, spend time with my kids, go out with my husband, and be involved in my aging mom's care. Over time, I learned to value my time as much as my money.

> I had to learn to value my time as much as my money.

Time Is a Valuable Commodity

Like many of us, nonprofits tend to value money but not time. Their staff tends to work too many hours and think they have endless amounts of time. They're tight with the money but not the time. Perhaps they don't realize that time is a valuable commodity.

What if we started valuing our time the way we value money? What if we watched every minute, discussed how each hour was spent, and assessed the success of a project based on the time expended as a measure of the results?

Because I'm a consultant and get paid by the hour, I have a habit of logging my hours, and I suggest you do the same. Everyone who charges for their time has a method of logging their hours. This isn't a foreign concept. But it *is* foreign to nonprofits, which typically don't consider their time as valuable enough to track. This is yet another indication of codependence—we don't think of our time as having worth. But time isn't an endless commodity. How we spend it is worthy of our attention.

I get a lot of pushback when I suggest that nonprofit staff log how they spend their time, so I know I hit a nerve. When I bring this up at workshops or seminars, my attendees get hot! They insist there are many reasons why they can't track their time. Here are some of the popular arguments:

- I work on three projects in fifteen minutes. How am I supposed to track that?

- I'm constantly interrupted. How can I track that time?

- I may talk to one person in one conversation about three projects. How do I track that?

OK, everyone—off the ledge! This isn't that hard. Having an *idea* of how your time is spent is better than nothing. Tracking things minute by minute may not be necessary.

Like anything else, change is hard until we see the benefits. So let's find out how tracking time can benefit you.

Time Should Be Counted Against the Bottom Line

Imagine a special event. Let's say you have a lovely dinner auction and lots of people come. You have honorary chairs, a volunteer committee, and a staff to support the event. The event raises about thirty thousand dollars, which is a nice chunk of change.

But what did that event really cost? How many staff hours went into raising that money? Let's say one staff person who makes forty thousand dollars managed the event. All said and done, it took four months to plan and about three hundred total hours of their time, which averages to about eighteen hours a week for that four months. That's about seven thousand dollars of staff time to plan the event.

If that time could have been spent engaged in other activities, then that time should be charged against the event. Same with newsletters, the website, social media, and everything else.

The best thing you can do to understand the worth of your communications is to track your hours. Assess how much what you do costs in terms of time *and* money and to measure the results on both those factors.

> The best thing you can do to understand the worth of your communications is to track your hours.

Let me tell you something else: when you don't value your time, it results in burnout, bad feelings, and lack of productivity. I recently met Beth Kanter, who, along with Aliza Sherman, wrote a fabulous book on self-care in nonprofits called *The Happy, Healthy Nonprofit: Strategies for Impact Without Burnout.*

Burnout in nonprofits is a real thing, and it's a problem. And the attitude of "oh, we have all this time" contributes to it. Are you overworked? Not enough time in the day? Feel like you can't get ahead? These can all be addressed through better time management. But before you can manage your time, you have to understand how you're spending it. Start tracking your time.

Prioritize

How can you prioritize your time to focus on what really matters without getting distracted by what doesn't, in order to be as productive as possible? How can you find the time for marketing that matters?

1. Spend Your Time on Building Relationships

Stop spending time on things that don't build relationships. Staff time is best spent doing the things that no one else can do—building relationships with those who care about you and attracting new like-minded people.

My friend and longtime colleague Amy Cole Buehler told me that as a fundraising consultant, she wishes that raising money and marketing were kept separate. As a marketing person, I didn't understand. Marketing supports fundraising, so how can we separate the two? Her philosophy: development people often use marketing activities as an excuse to feel like they're asking for money, but that's not what they're doing. Too many of them hide behind activities like developing newsletters, brochures, etc., when they should be developing relationships and getting new donors.

2. Ditch the Bad Ideas and Filter the New Ones

About four years ago, I took over Thanksgiving from my mother. She was getting older and had moved to a small apartment. Since I have the biggest house in the family, it seemed logical that I host family parties.

The first year was rough. My husband and I, with help from my brother and sister-in-law, figured out how to have a seated dinner for thirty in my dining room. Moving the chairs, prepping linens, china, and all the details—listen, I love this stuff, but it's a lot of work. When it's over, it takes me two to three days to recover!

But then I'd head into Christmas and think I was going to get the same amount of stuff done before I became Queen of Thanksgiving. I soon realized I was taking the "pile on" approach. I had a new responsibility, and instead of reviewing my current responsibilities and seeing what I could let go of or diminish, I just piled it on. That lasted a few years, and I always entered the Christmas holiday completely exhausted.

Now I know that I can't do everything I did before I started hosting Thanksgiving. I also know which aspects of the holidays are important to me and my family, and I stick to those things. I let go of most of the shopping and leave it to my husband. I let go of making cookies, except very simple ones my kids like to make.

Nothing has to be perfect, which is huge for me. Absolutely huge. One day, my therapist told me that it's OK to be average at some things, and I was like, "NO IT IS NOT!" I thought I had to be spectacular at everything. Now I'm spectacular at things I care about, like the fabulous White Christmas party I throw every year, and I'm OK with being average at others, like baking.

Some years ago, the world changed dramatically, and we now have all these new ways of communicating. Adding social media was like me hosting Thanksgiving. Instead of rethinking all of our communications activities and making adjustments, we just piled on the new stuff. *Oh, now I have to do Instagram. Thanks, I was just finding the time to manage Facebook!*

This "pile it on" mentality is part of our codependence. We're afraid to ask for help—or to even ask to lighten our load. Oh, how we want to please!

Here's how we can really be pleasers: use our time and money most effectively to get attention to find long-term supporters and raise money. That's our goal. An assessment will help us understand what's working and what isn't.

And having plans helps us say "no." When board members come up with an idea—*let's do an event, let's have an auction, why aren't we doing this activity or that social media platform*—you can say, "Well, it's not in the plan." It's the plan that says no, not you. Plans help us filter big ideas. Plans help us stay on track and keep us focused on our goals.

Stop piling on. Find out what's working, and let go of what's not.

For Further Thought

- There are many free resources you can use to track your time and the time of your staff. Which one will you use?

- Name some things that you're currently doing that you could give up.

- What have you "piled on" that you can reevaluate?

Put It into Practice

As I was in the final stages of writing this book, it occurred to me that some people will like it and some won't. I'll have to use the techniques I've described in this book to manage praise and criticism for my own work. I know there'll be days when the criticism will hurt, but I also know I have the tools to move through it and keep moving forward. And if I get criticized, at least I said something interesting enough to make it comment-worthy!

Put It Into Practice

What about you? How can you implement the principles of courageous communication in your organization?

Step 1: Assessment

I've talked about assessment in almost every chapter, but it really is key. You need data to help you understand your effectiveness and your worth. And how do you do this?

List every marketing activity you do that supports fundraising or programs including your website, publications, and events. If you are a big agency, you may need to do this with others. If you are small, you most likely can do it yourself. Answer these questions:

- What are the goals of each activity?

- What is the cost of each activity?

- How much time does it take your staff to do each activity and what are your internal costs?

- How do you measure success?

- How successful are you in meeting the goals?

- What is working; what is not working?

- What can you live without? What should you be doing more of?

- What are three to five benefits of courageous communication to your organization?

- What are your top five concerns?

This is going to take you a bit of time, but it's worth it. You need a starting point for change, and you'll need data to support the change.

I very much believe in the idea of organizational codependence, but when you first bring it up, some will roll their eyes at this kind of talk. We must not dismiss our naysayers because those eye rolls aren't necessarily what you think they might be. Most likely, they're disguising the fear of making bad decisions. Remember, courageous communication requires accepting that things are scary but using rational thinking rather than fear to make decisions. An assessment like this can help you address the need for change.

Step 2: Slow Your Roll

I want this book to amaze and inspire you, but I also want you to take it slow. Change is scary, and it takes time. I know you are fired up and excited—or at least I hope you are—but please realize that others aren't with you yet. Share the book, but also slowly share your thoughts.

You also need to check your own ability to manage praise and criticism. If it's hard for you to manage criticism, read *Codependent No More: How to Stop Controlling Others and Start Caring for Yourself* by Melanie Beattie. This book can help you understand codependence and how it affects your life.

Step 3: Start at the Top

Branding begins with the brand promise—what is it that you want to change? What promise do you offer to those who interact with you? This is a fundamental and you have to get it right before you do anything else. And then it becomes your tagline, description, and talking points. Don't start in the middle.

Step 4: Be a Consensus Builder

People like to be included in the process, and since branding is the work of everyone in the organization, it helps to have a representative process. This isn't something for you to churn out at your desk.

Many years ago, a nonprofit moved into a new building and they decided to change their visual brand. One of their board members went off on their own and designed a new logo and new color scheme. When I tell you that the employees were in tears because they hated it so much, I'm not lying.

But then I stepped back and asked, "What can I learn from this?" First of all, the board member designed something without any input from staff, which meant he was working in a vacuum. Second, the staff was not prepared for the visual change, and the move had already put them in a place of high stress. Third, the change was rolled out with little fanfare, and it took the staff by surprise.

Before you make any decisions, get input, reassure those involved that the changes are in their best interest and done with their needs in mind, and don't take anyone by surprise. If people aren't included in the process, they feel threatened. An inclusive process means less hurdles later.

Step 5: Put Your House in Order

Brand promise, tagline, description, talking points, supporting data all have to come in order, one after another. What do you stand for? What's your passion? What change do you seek?

Push your messaging as far as you can. Be bold, be brave, be controversial—which means *be interesting*. It's easier to pull back than to start safe and have it end there.

When we named a new campaign for Lutheran Foundation of Saint Louis, they were scared of the change. This campaign's brand was different from their usual traditional image. The campaign encouraged congregations to get involved in social service outreach, so the message didn't need to resonate with foundation executives but with people in pews.

The campaign theme, "Serve Boldly," was a bold choice for them. It was different, but it was supposed to be different.

This was their way to show they were accessible, interested, and willing to fund new projects and train volunteers. There were a few "deep breath" moments, but we always brought it back to this: this is not about your comfort but the comfort of our audiences. "Serve Boldly" was a hit, and the campaign continues to this day. It more than exceeded its goals. Was it scary? Yes. Was it successful? Heck yes!

Be bold. Be brave. Remember, no one ever got attention by being nice and safe. As I write this, there's a protest march in my neighborhood. I believe we are in a new civil rights movement, and we're beginning to understand why it's important to stand up for what we believe. It seems that with access to social media, criticism is all around us, and that's true. But that can't keep us from sharing our message because—remember—we cannot change minds; we can only attract like-minded people to us.

I will always be a codependent nightmare. The goal isn't to change that but to accept that it's the truth and to work with it. Try not to think of this as a cure for organizational codependence. It's a way for you to understand and manage your communications, make better decisions, and be stronger in your message, so you can attract like-minded, long-term, and dedicated supporters to your cause.

> Try not to think of this as a cure for organizational codependence. It's a way for you to understand and manage your communications, make better decisions, and be stronger in your message, so you can attract like-minded, long-term, and dedicated supporters to your cause.

You can do it! Be courageous!

About the Author

Maryanne Dersch has spent almost thirty years working in the nonprofit world, the last fifteen at *501creative*, where she helps clients reach their communication and branding goals. As resident extrovert at *501*, she gives workshops, writes copy, facilitates group discussions, and eats a lot of chicken breast lunches. Before joining *501creative*, Maryanne was a consultant at Vector Communications and the public relations officer for the City of University City.

She's been on enough boards and committees through the years to make herself crazy, including Community Service Public Relations Council and the Saint Louis Chapter of Association of Fundraising Professionals. She is on the board of Foster and Adoptive Care Coalition and has been a foster parent for Stray Rescue of Saint Louis for twenty years.

Maryanne graduated from the University of Missouri-Columbia in 1988 with a degree in journalism. There she learned to compose copy at the keyboard, meet a deadline, and recognize that stories are all around us. That's also when she started a long and prosperous relationship with both her husband and Truman the Tiger.

Maryanne and her husband, Jon Schmuke, have three children. She's known for her love of ultrahigh heels, extra-large Diet Cokes, and short karaoke rotations.

Made in the USA
Middletown, DE
27 May 2021